MOUNTS 5

Christmas Coloring Book

AUTHOR AND ILLUSTRATOR
OLGA GOLOVESHKINA

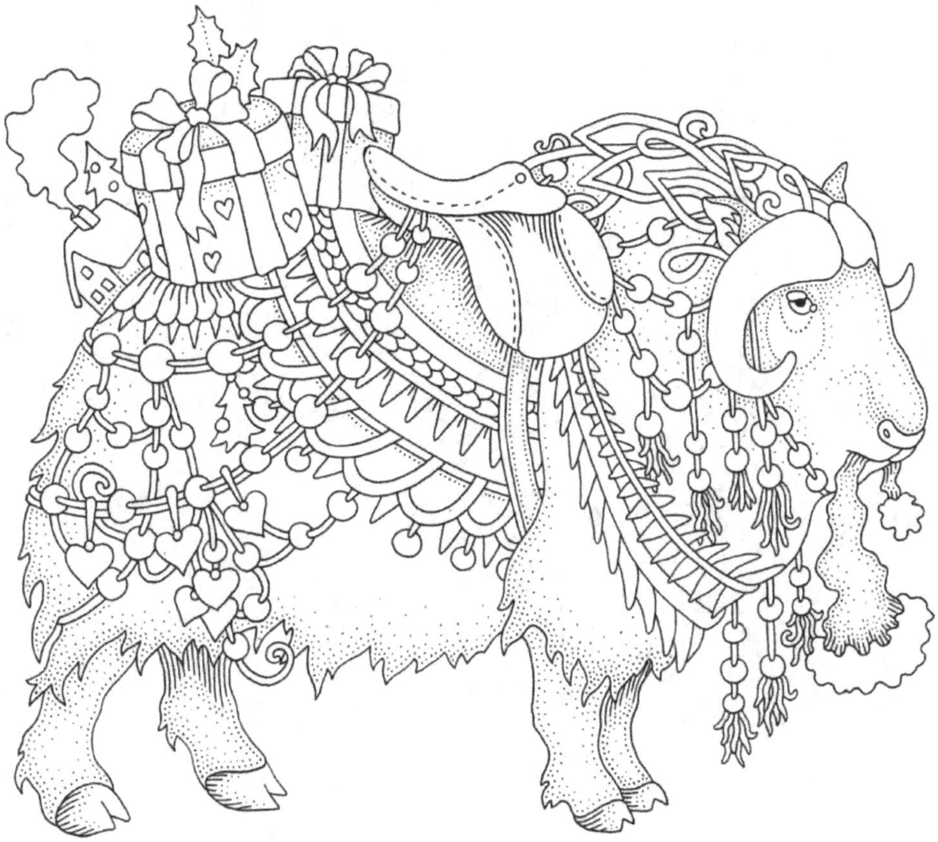

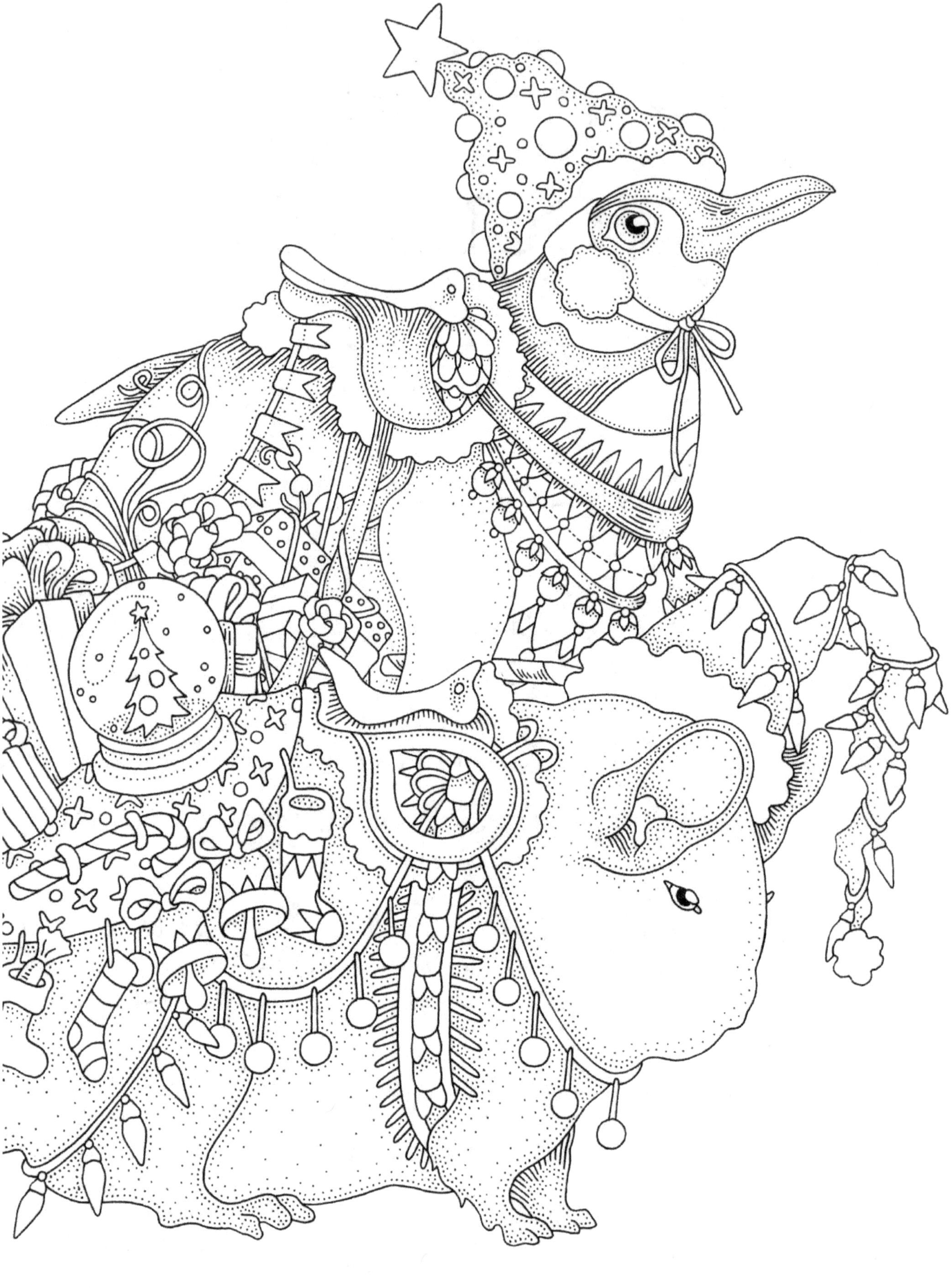

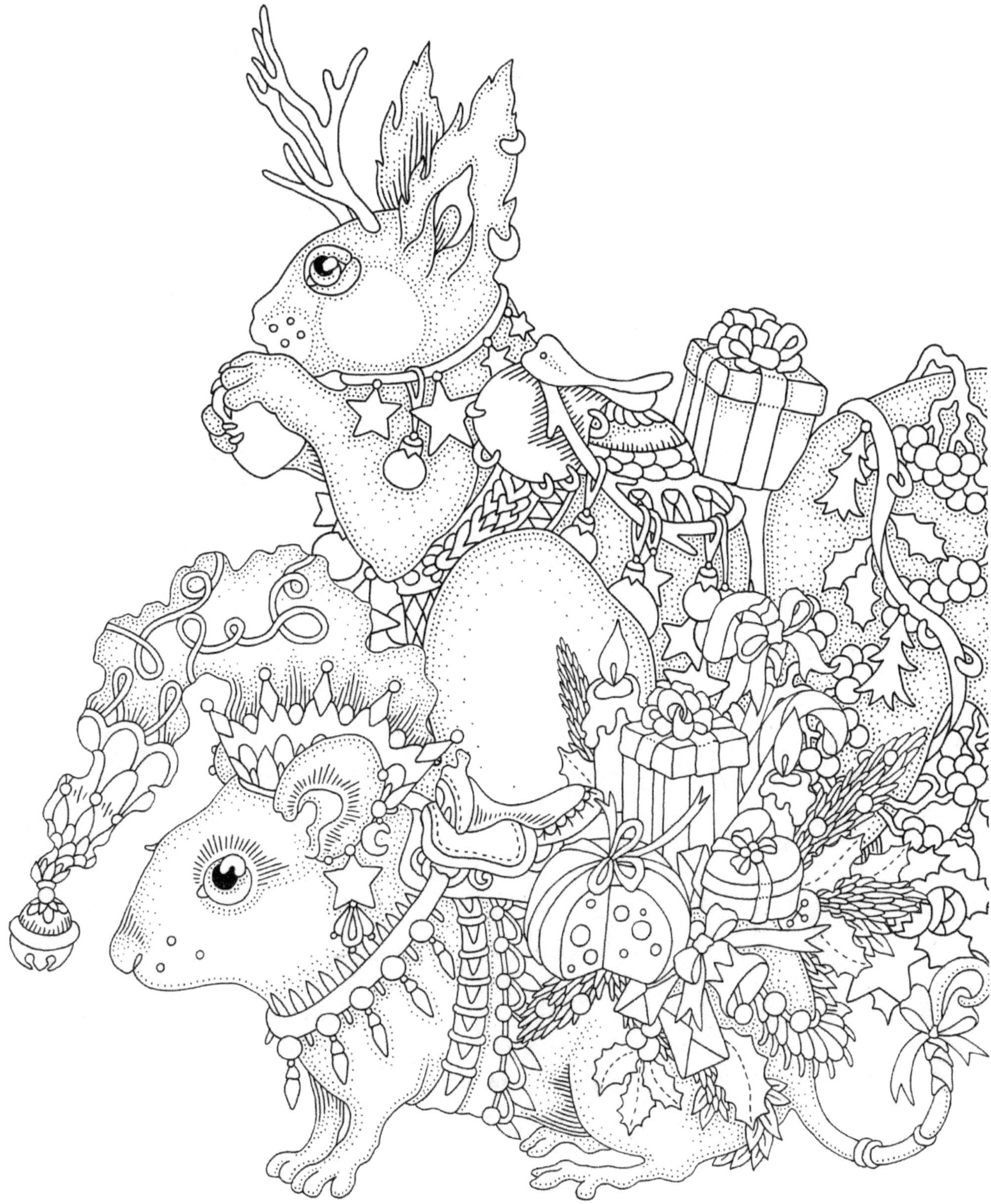

ISBN: 1979920206
ISBN-13: 9781979920209

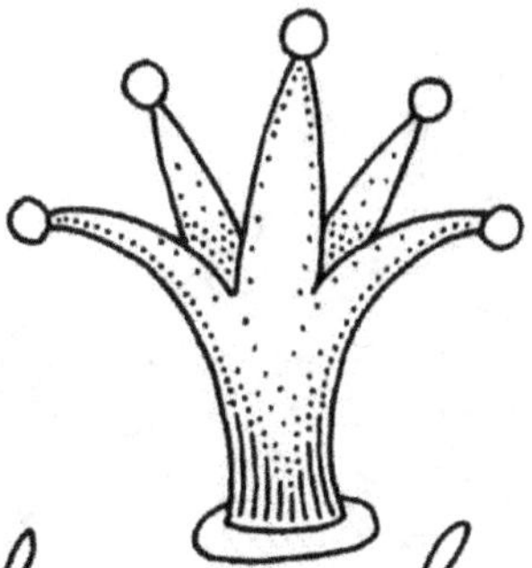

Happy coloring

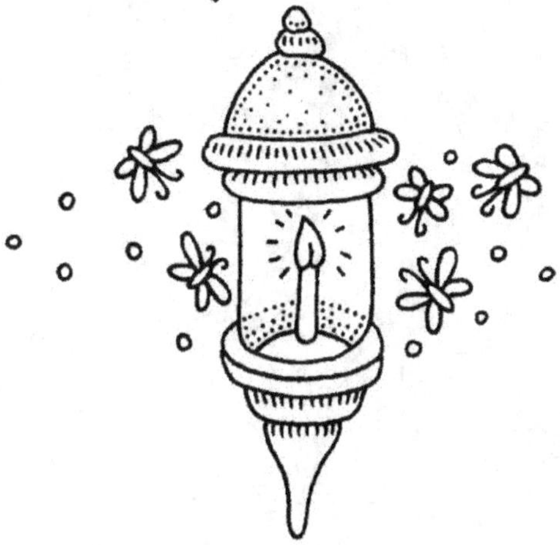

Thank you for choosing my coloring book!

Olya :)

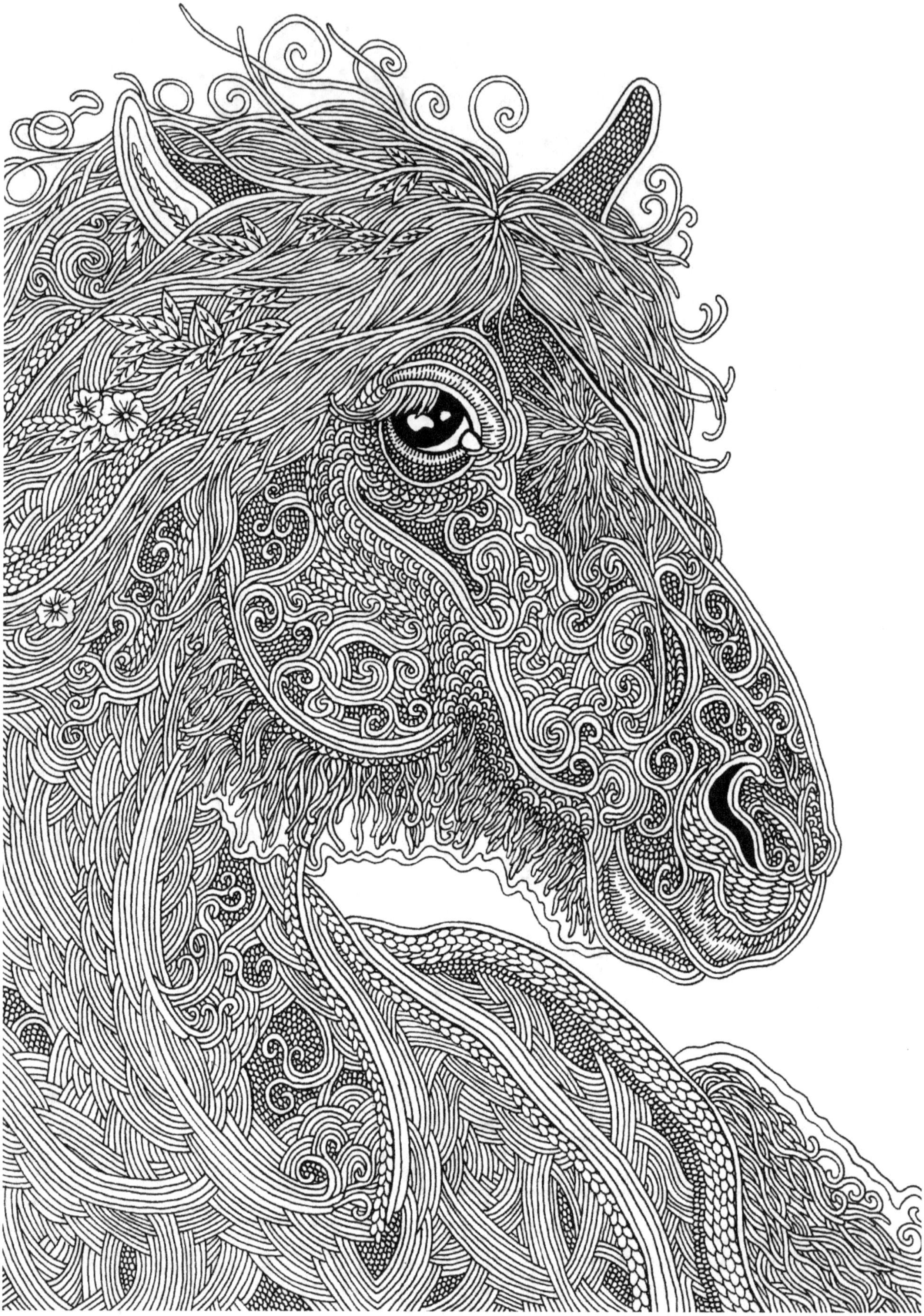

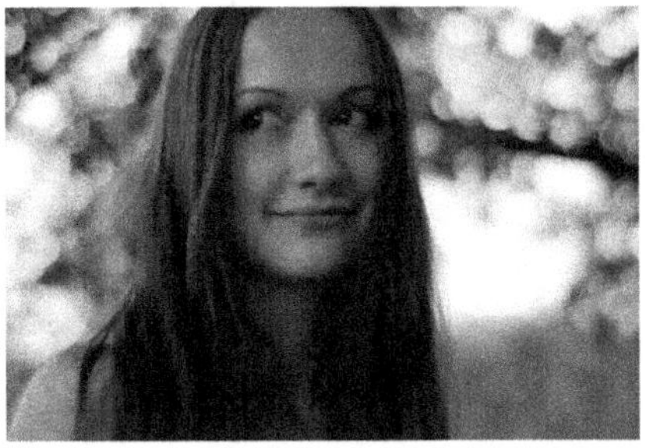

ABOUT THE AUTHOR

Olga Goloveshkina is a freelance artist and illustrator based in Moscow, Russia.
She graduated from the Institute of Business and Design.
Olga specializes in black ink doodles.
She is an author and illustrator coloring books for adults:

1. "The wind carries flowers"/"Veter unosit tsvety" (in Russian, 2015),
2. "Fox travel: Coloring book" (in English, 2016),
3. "Mounts" (in English, 2016),
4. "Mounts 2" (in English, 2016),
5. "Enchanted horses" (in English, 2016),
6. "Horse and Architecture" (in English, 2016),
7. "Alice in Wonderland Coloring Book" (in English, 2017),
8. "Mounts 3" zodiac coloring book (in English, 2017),
9. "Mounts 4" Halloween coloring book (in English, 2017),
10. "Mounts 5" Christmas coloring book (in English, 2017).

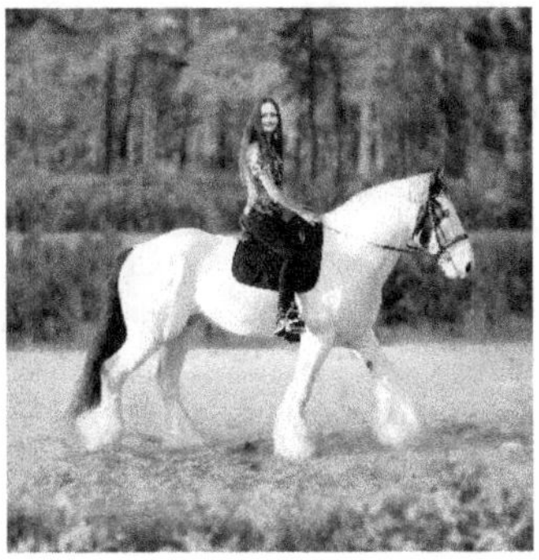

Author page on Amazon:

amazon.com/author/olgagoloveshkina

Site: http://olyagoloveshkina.jimdo.com

etsy.com/shop/OlyaColoringBook

Instagram:

@olyahitrayapanda

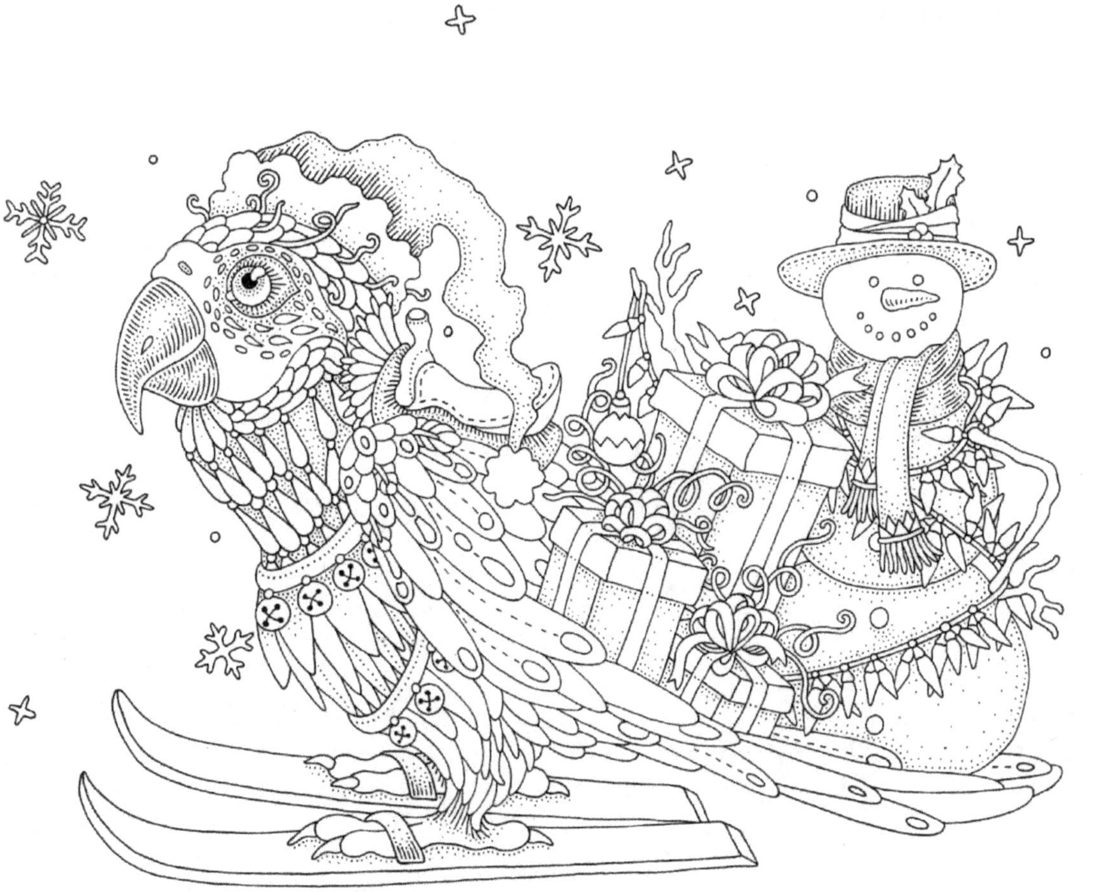

This book belongs to

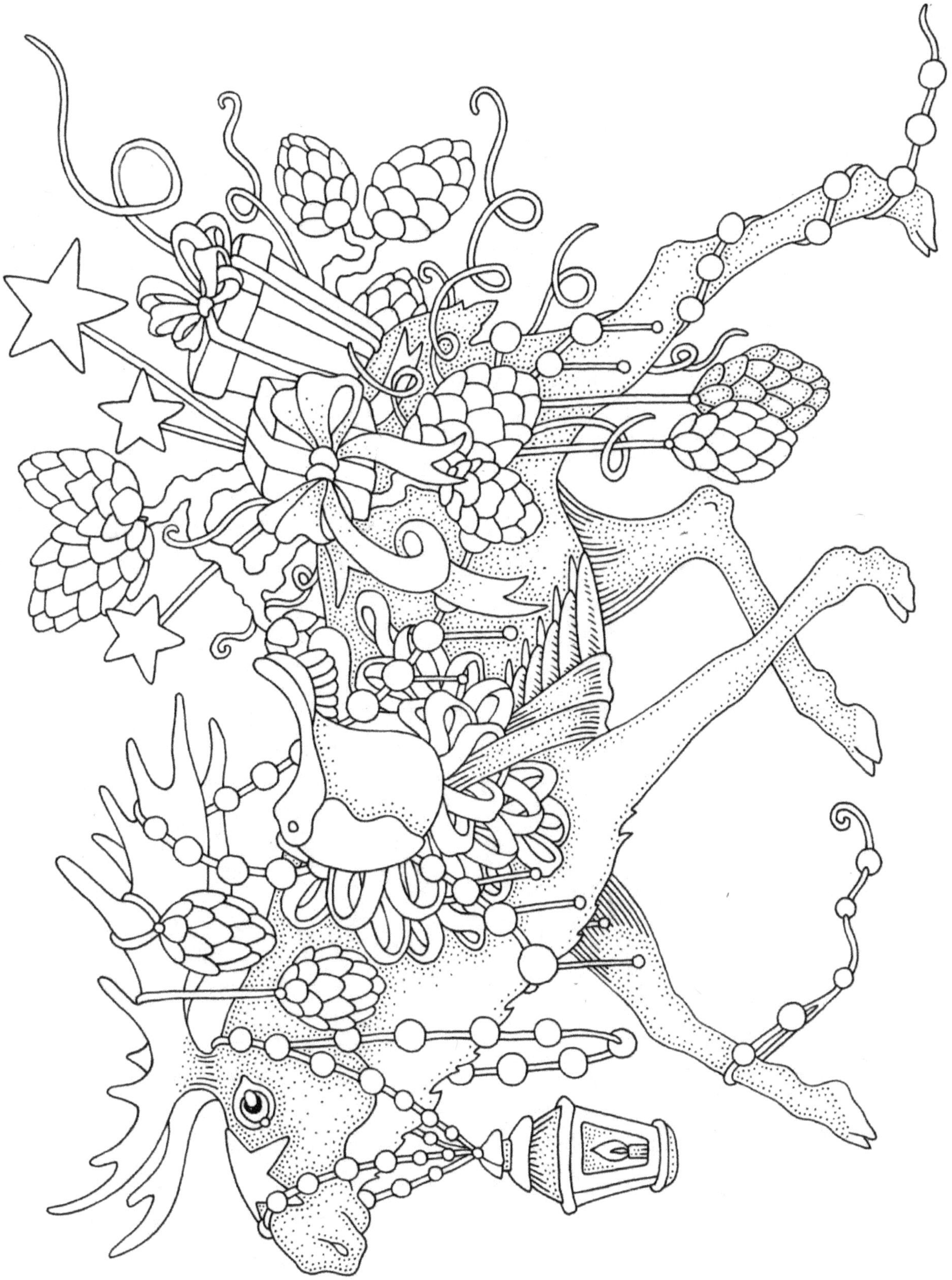

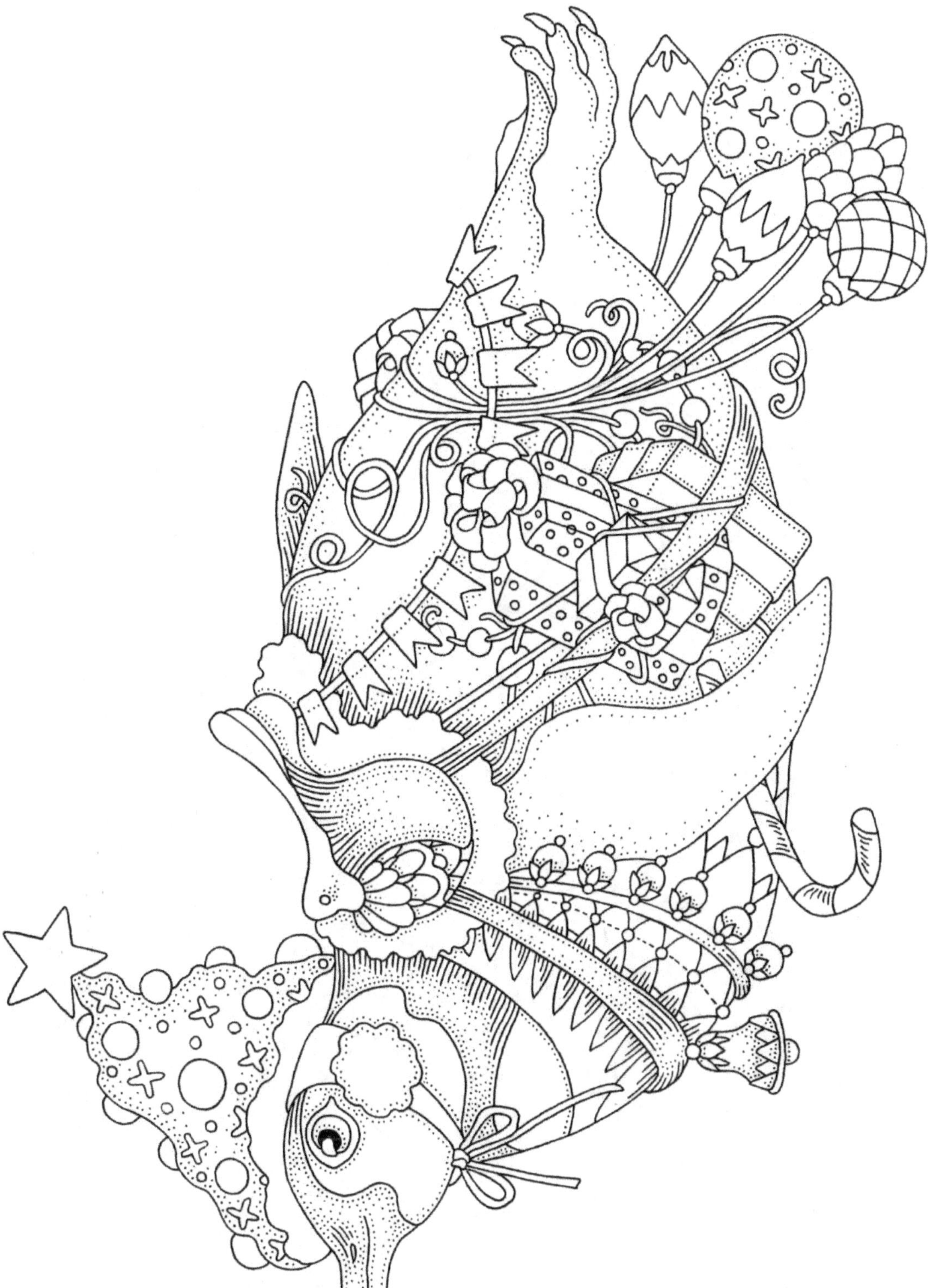

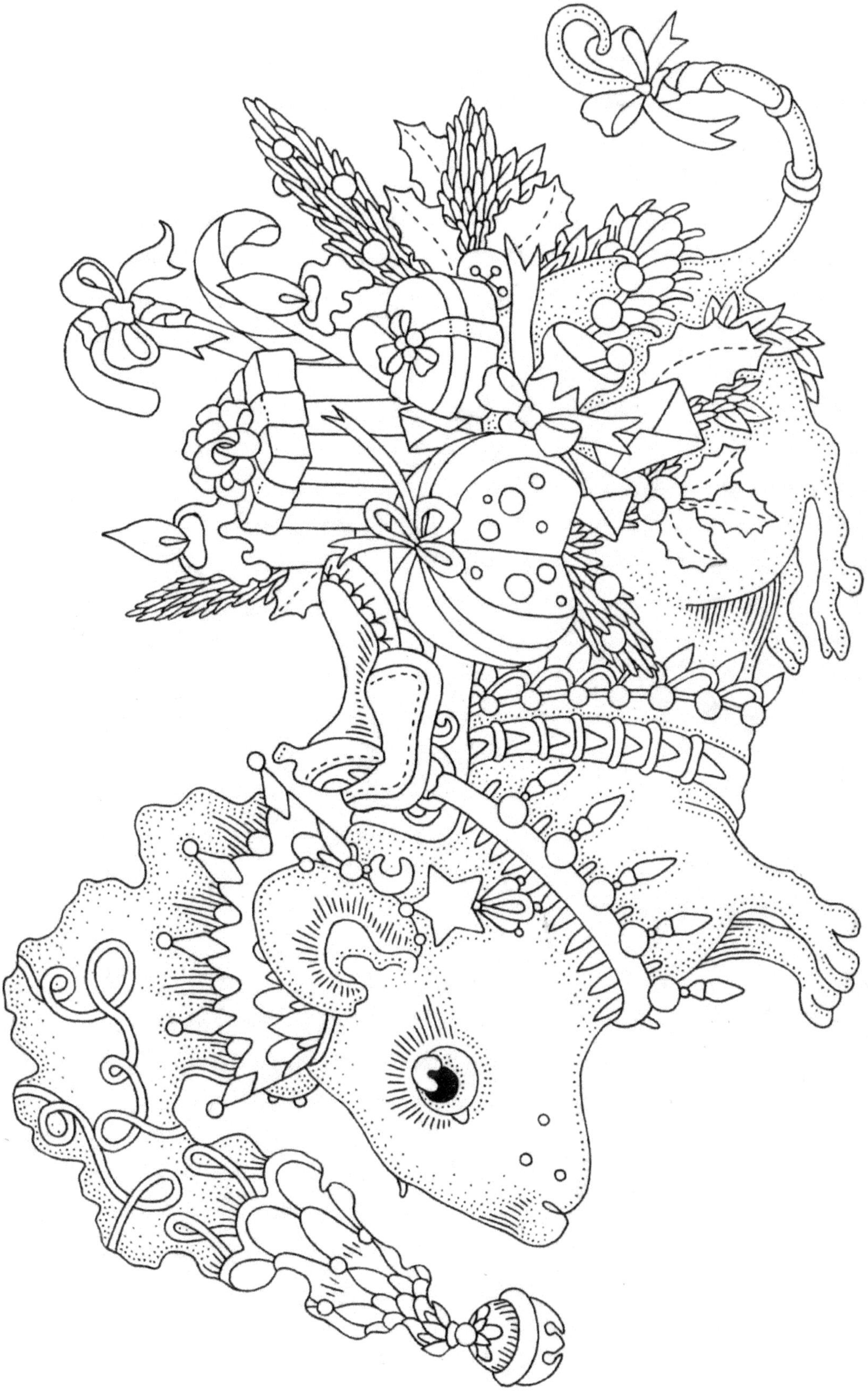

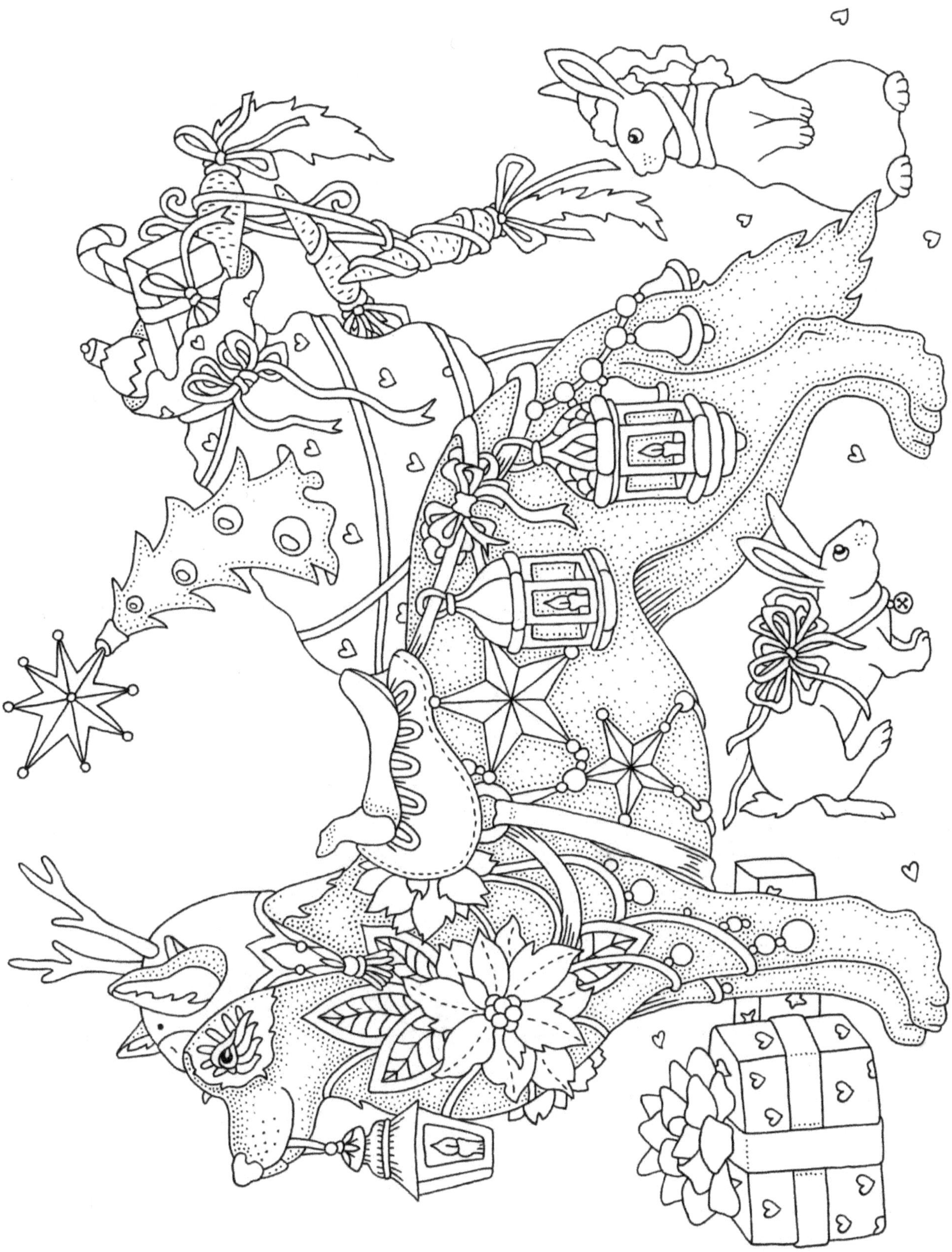

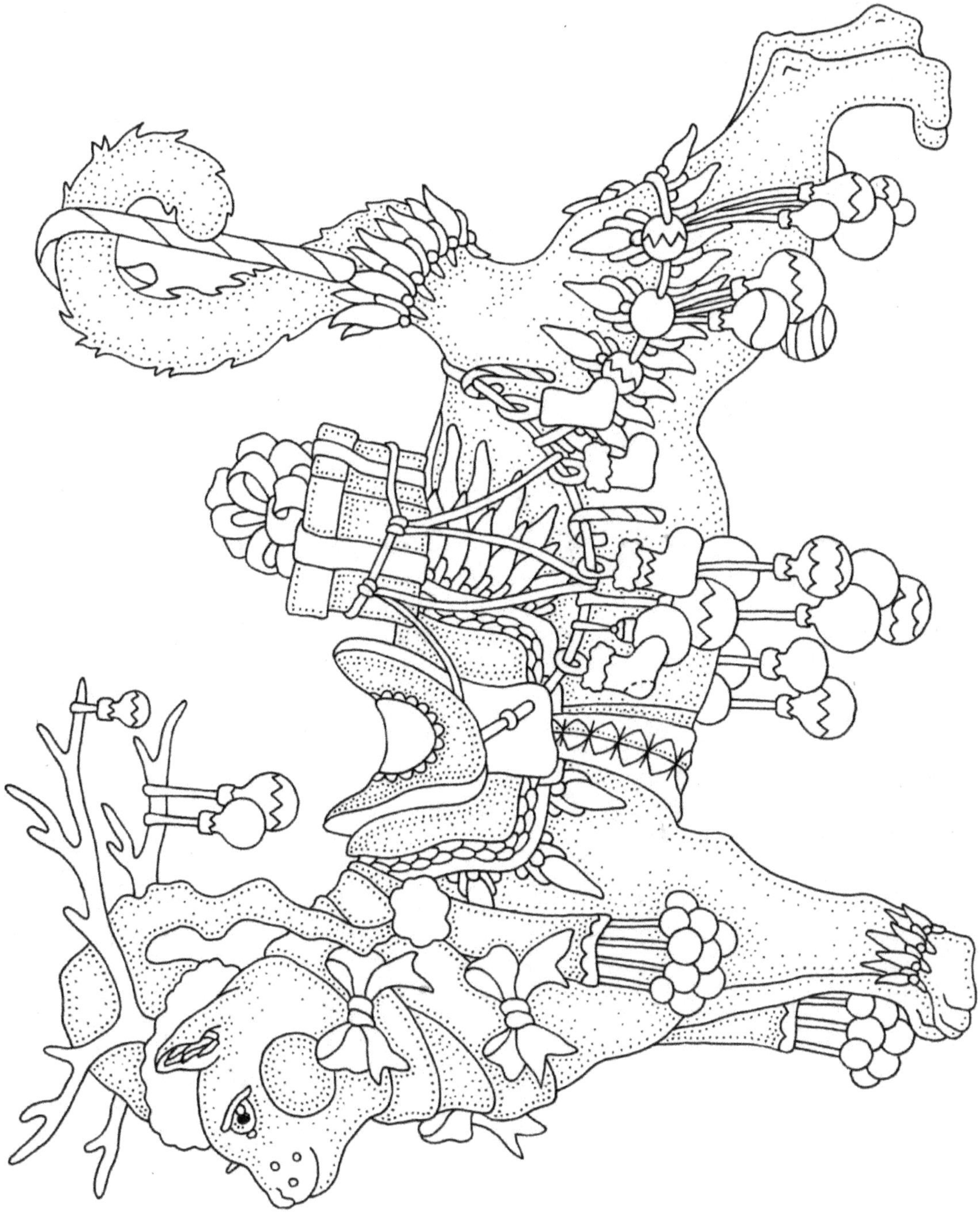

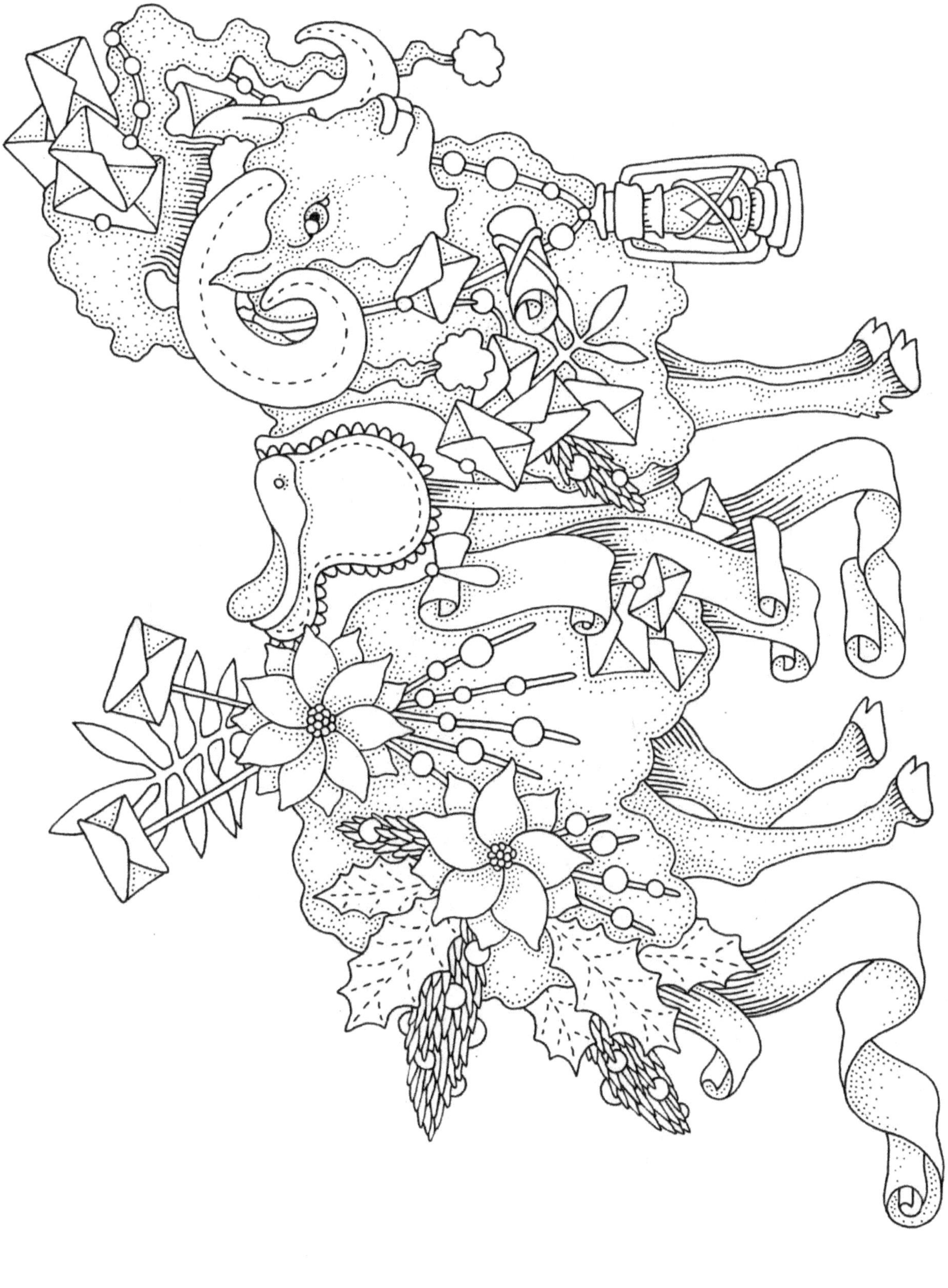

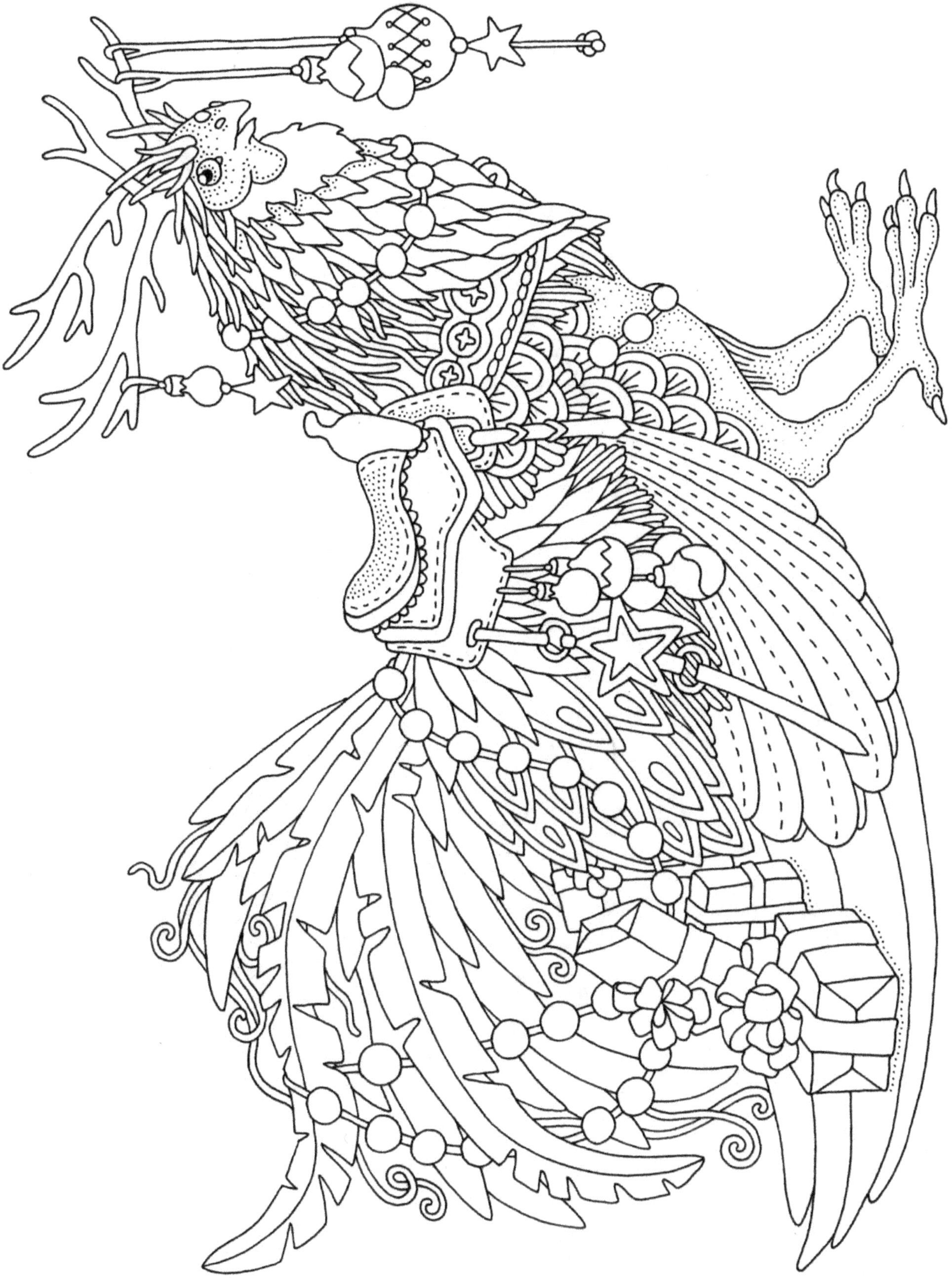

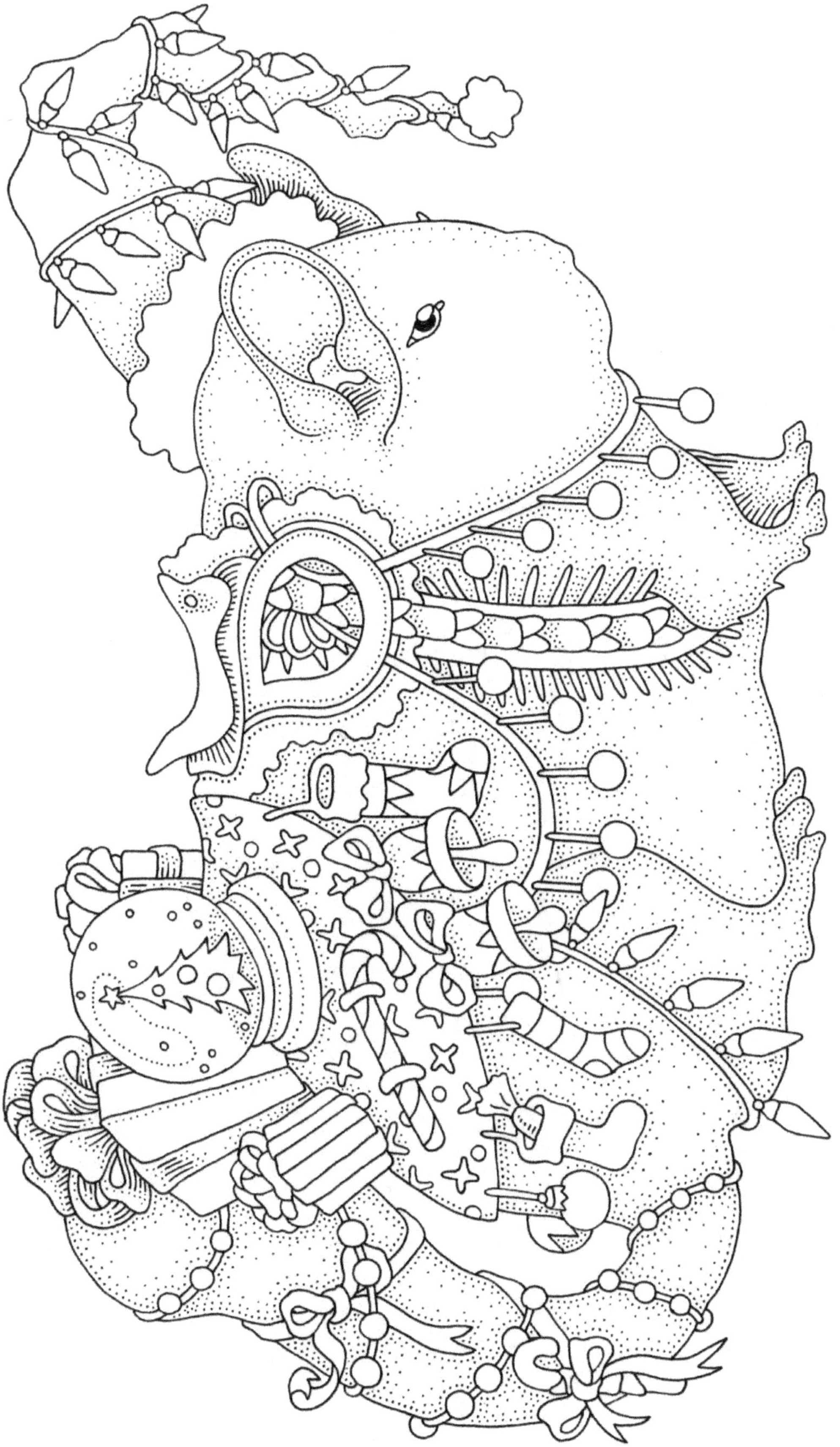

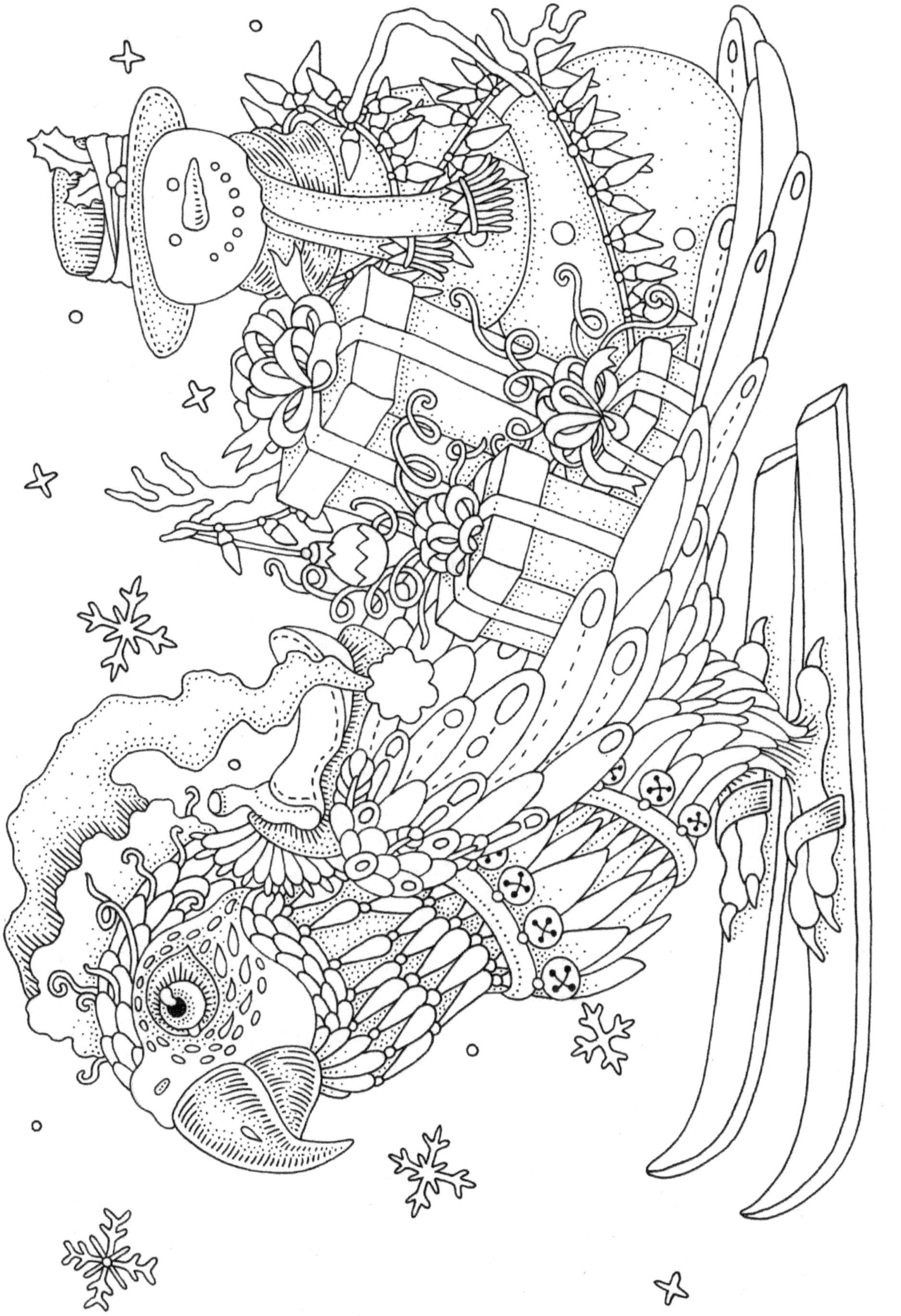

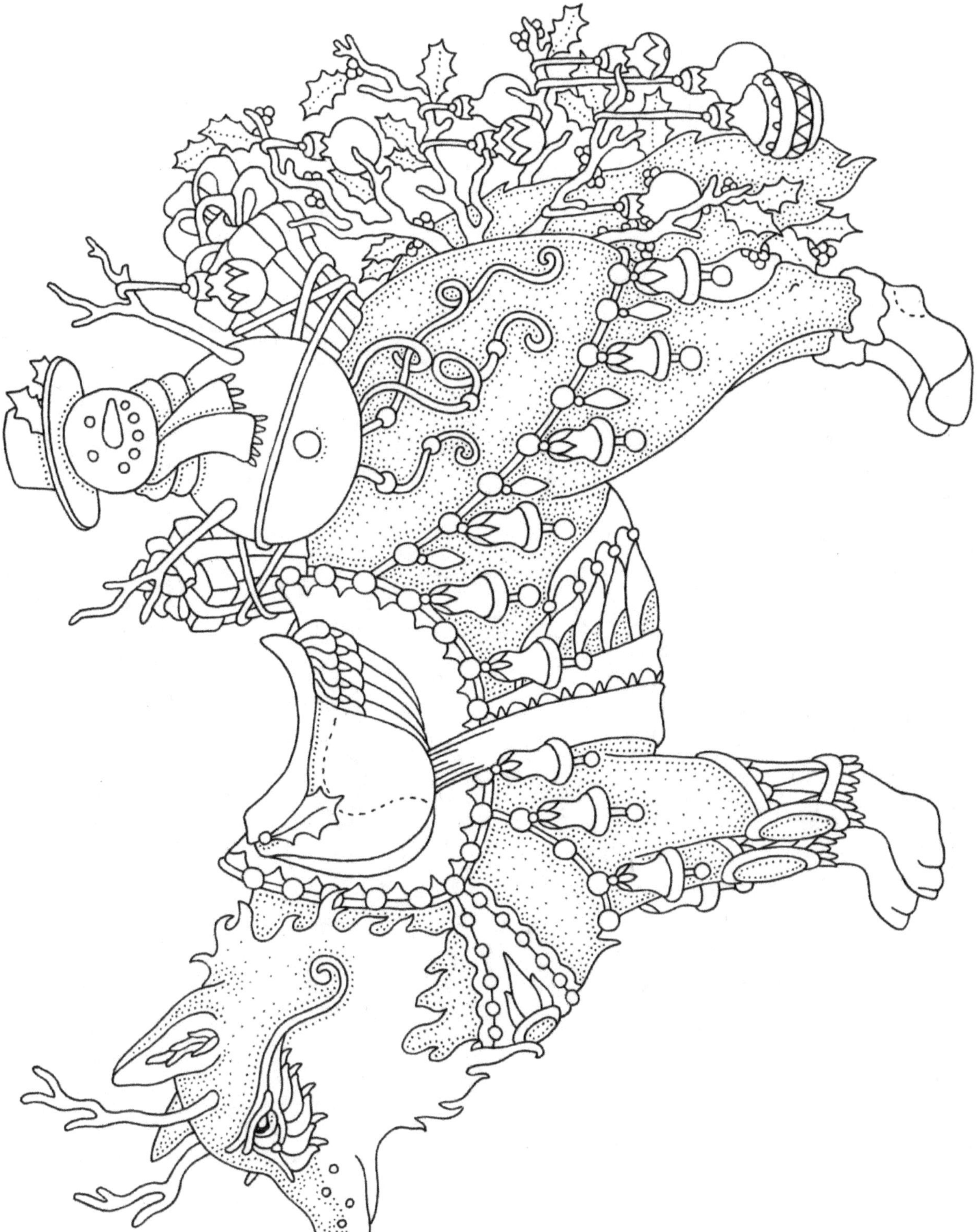

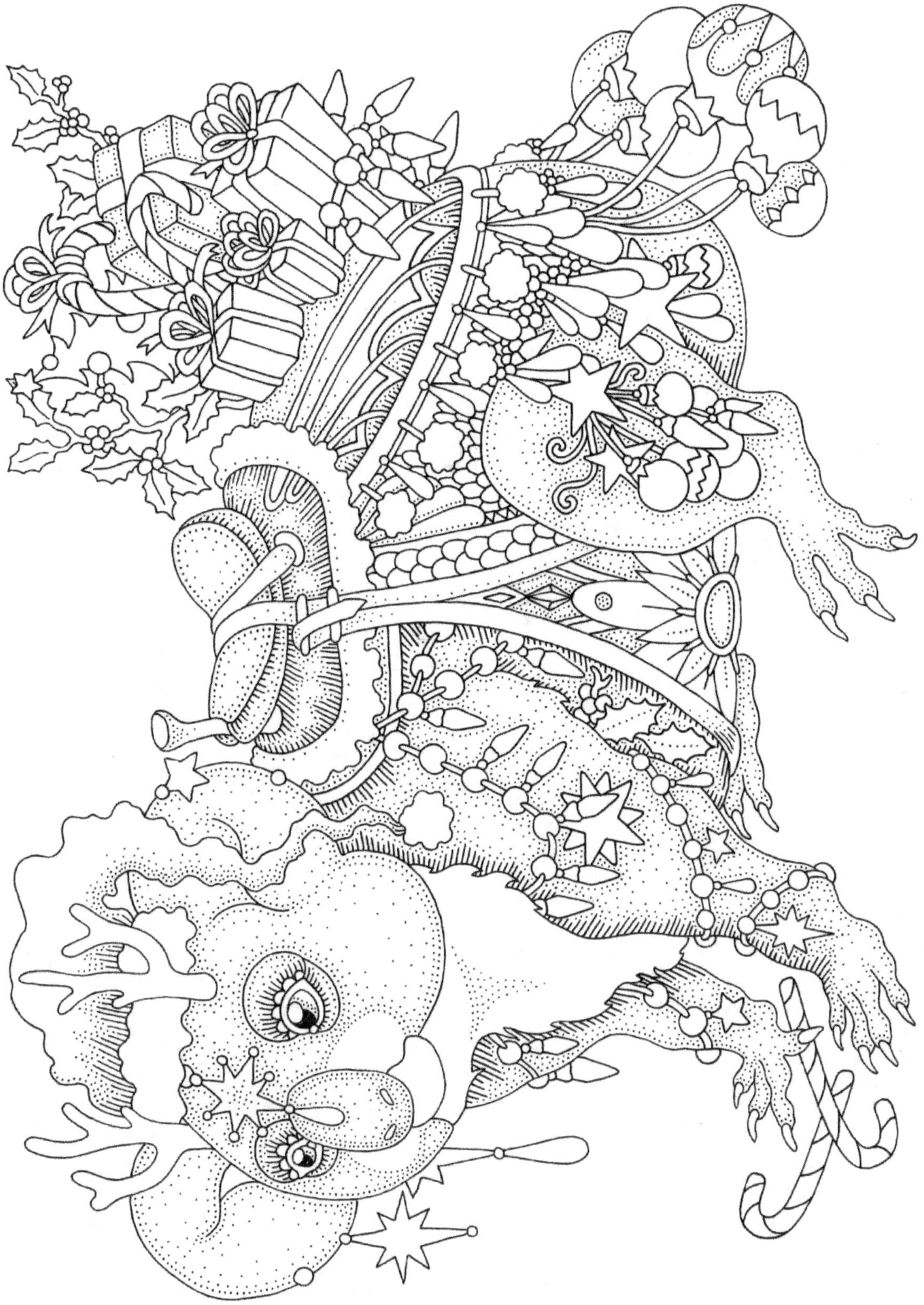

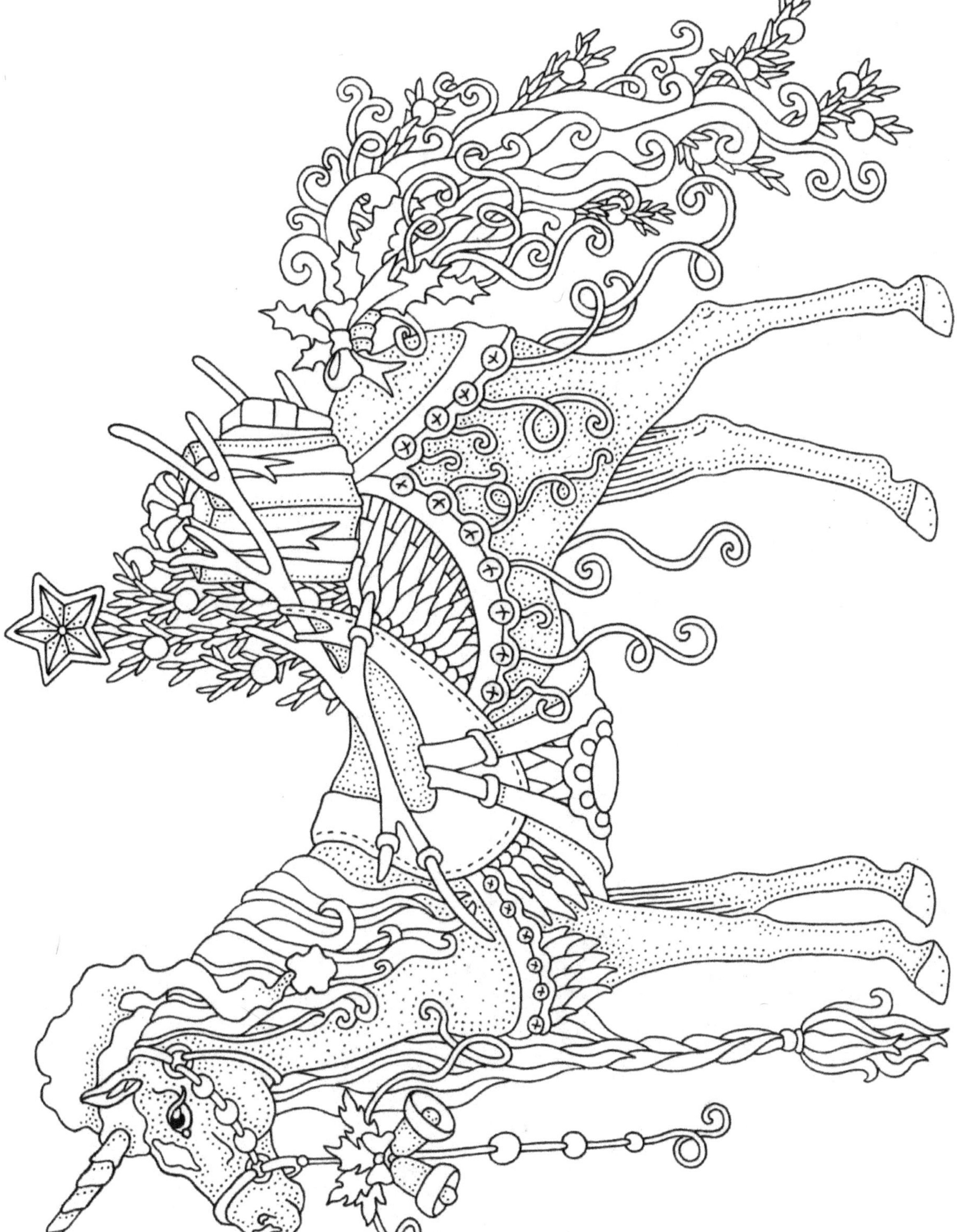

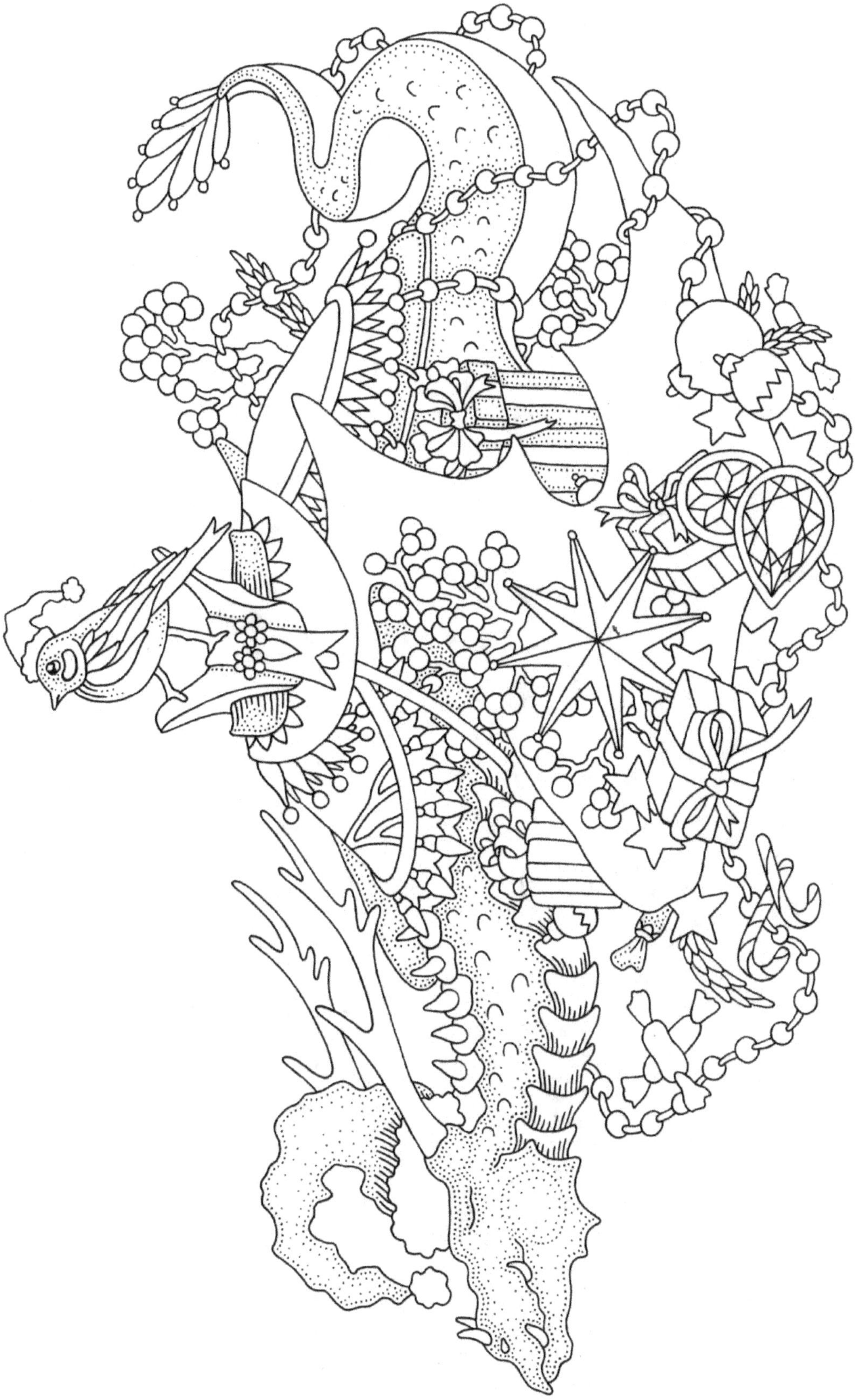

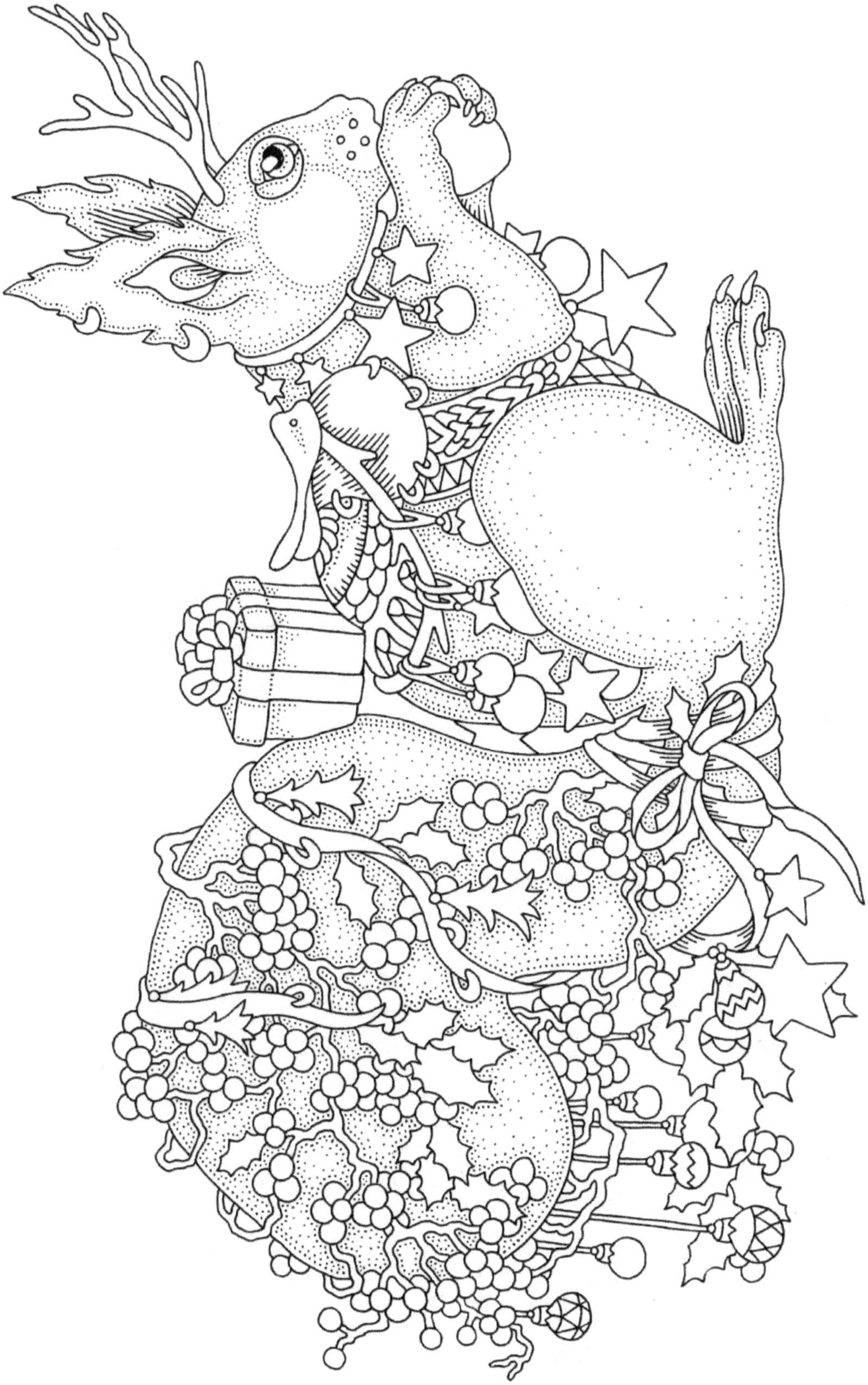

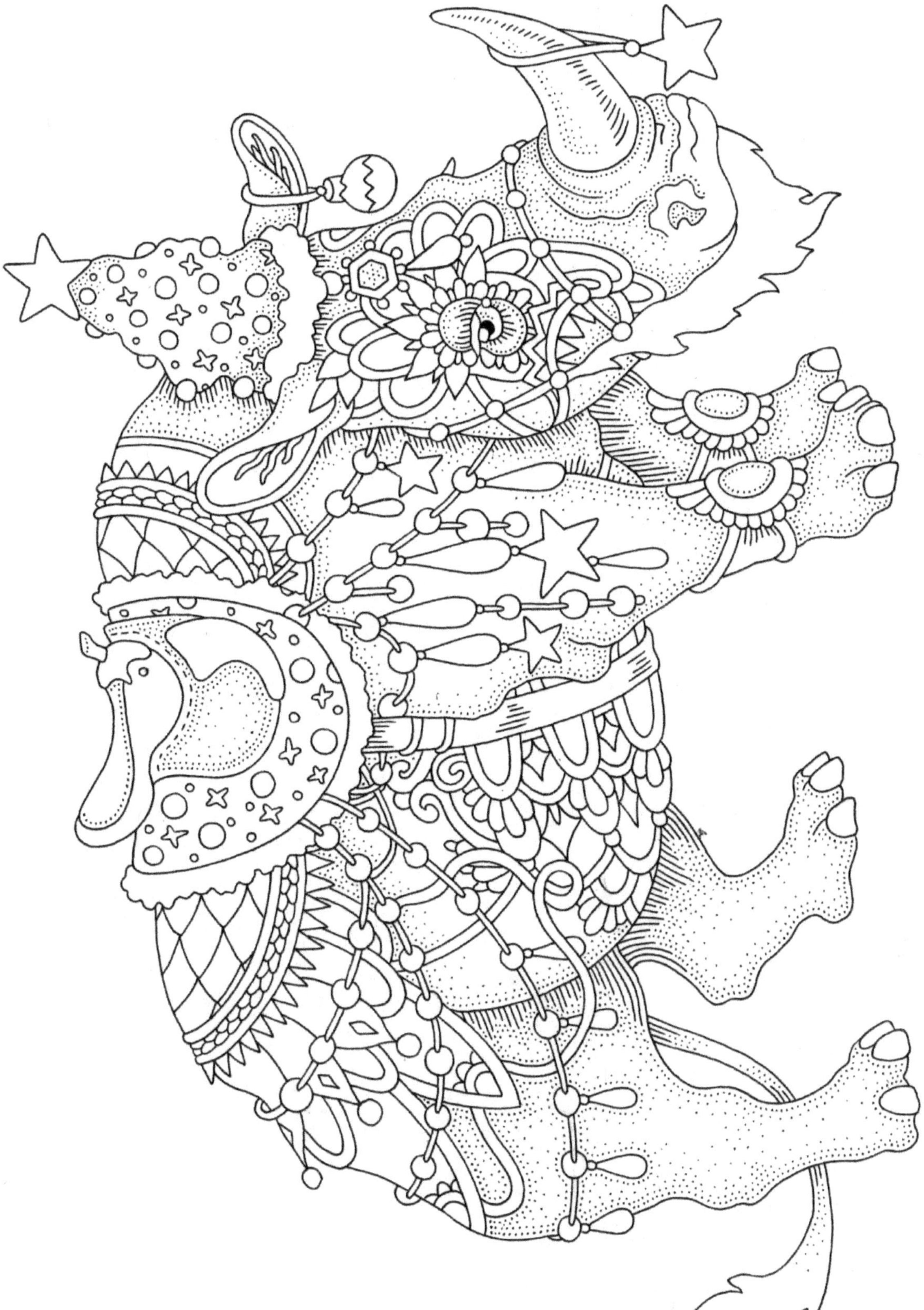

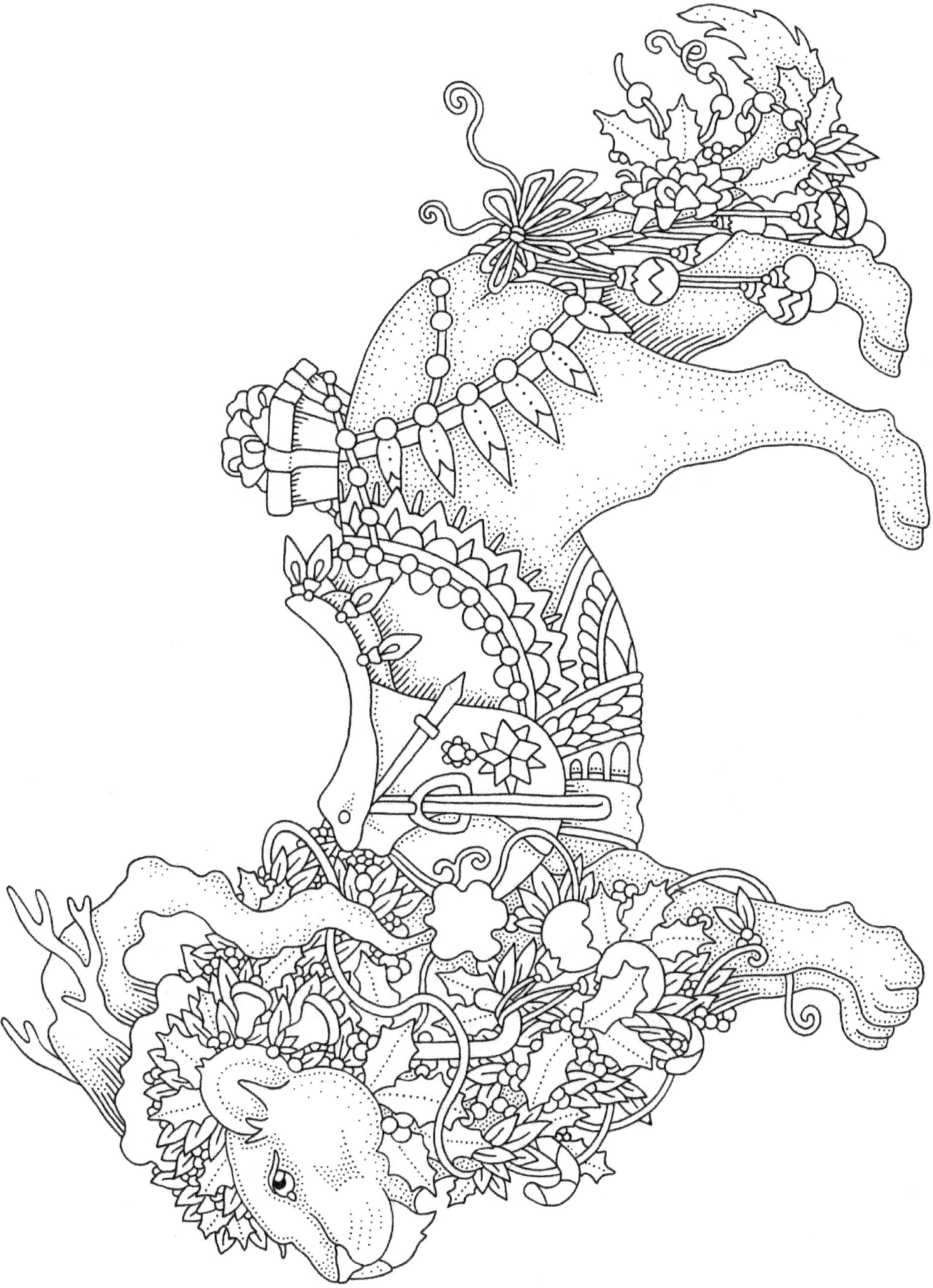

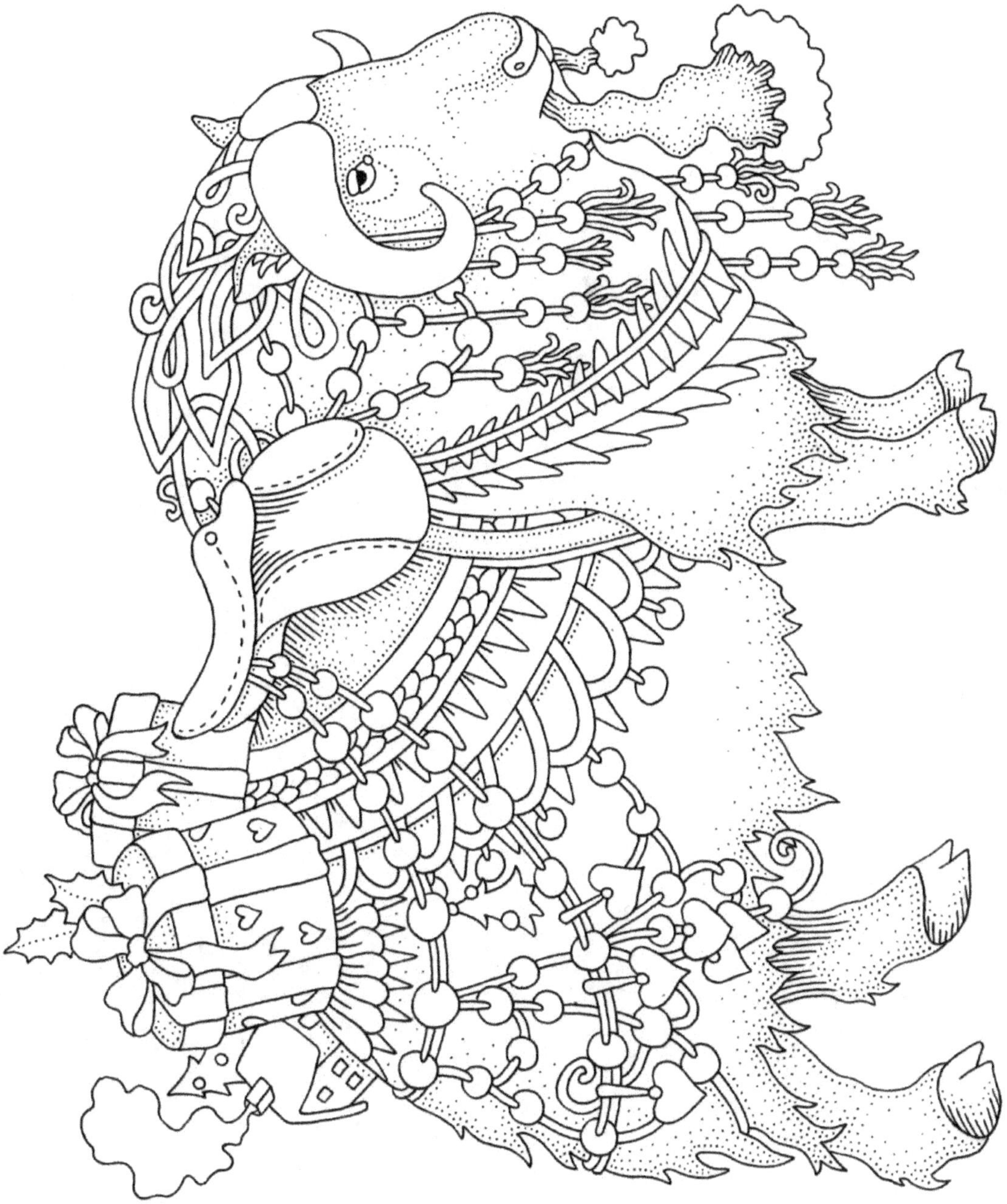

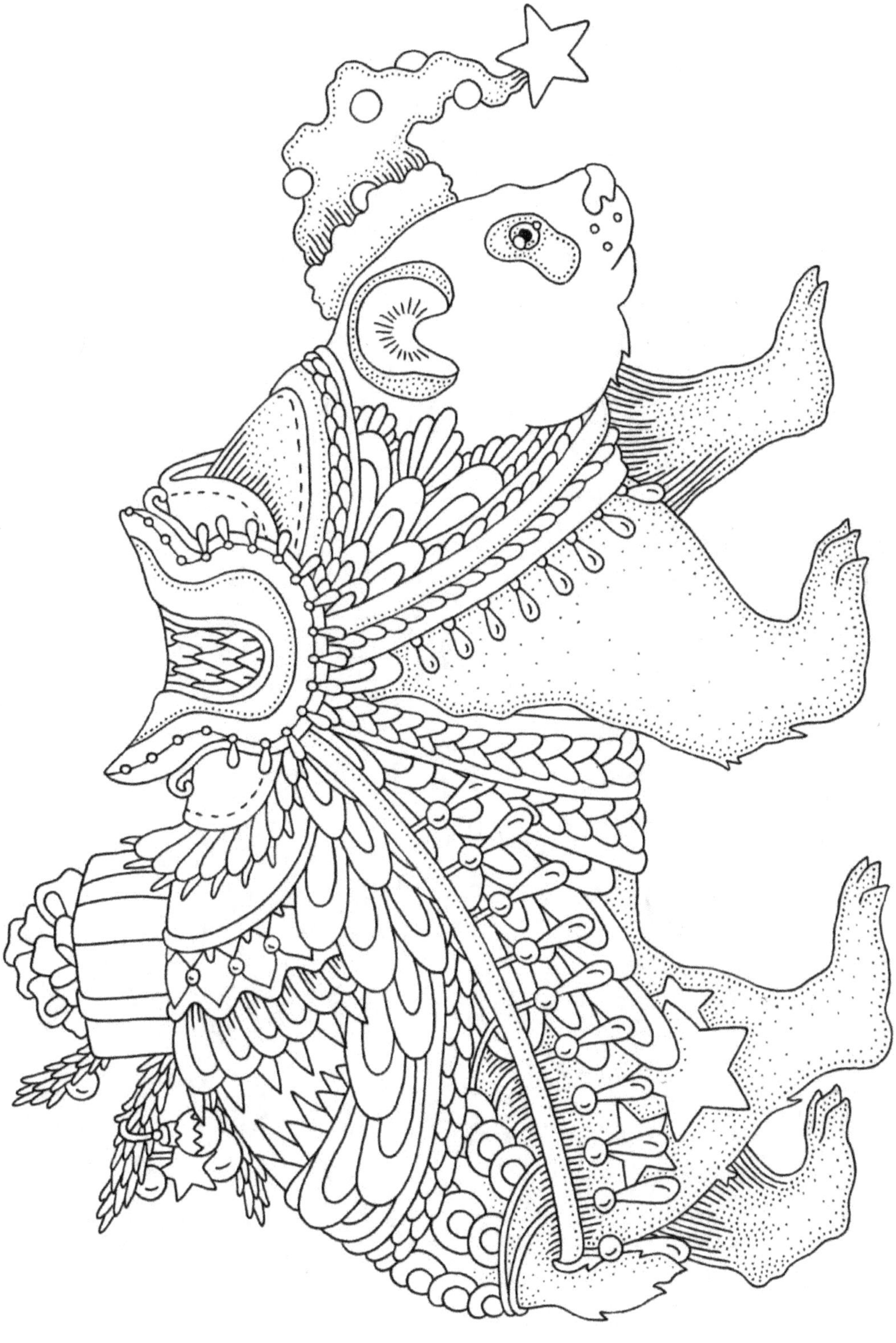

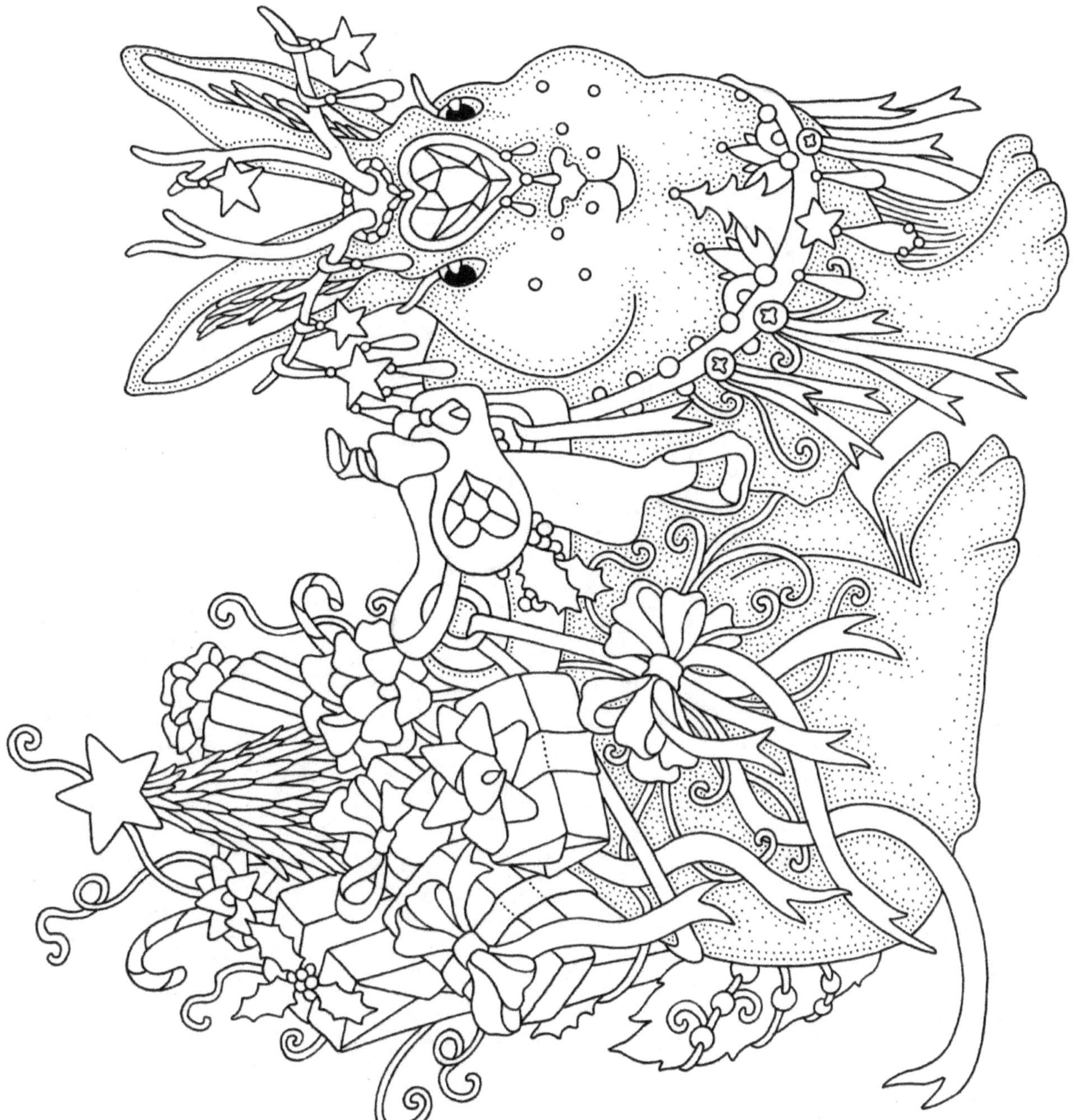

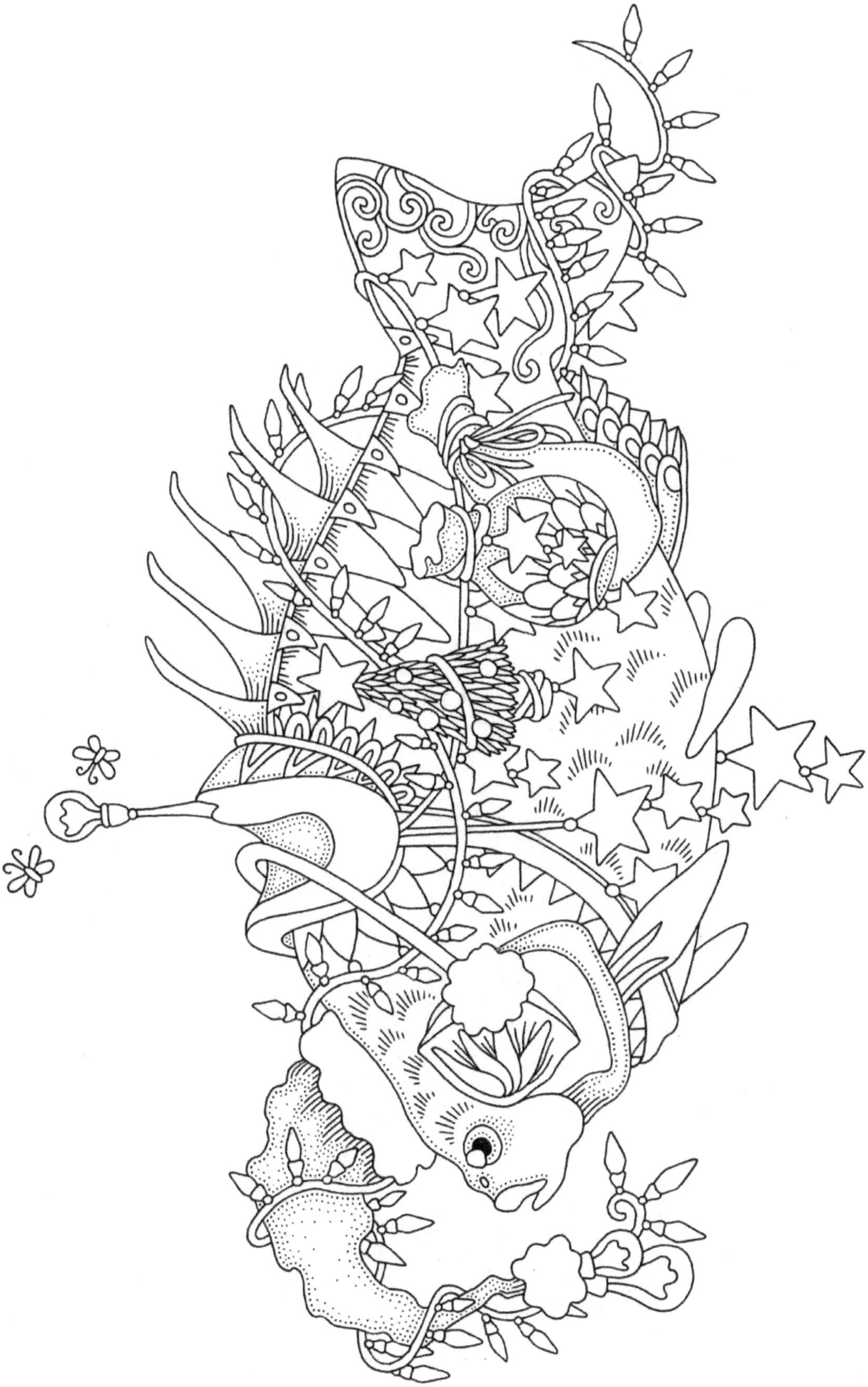

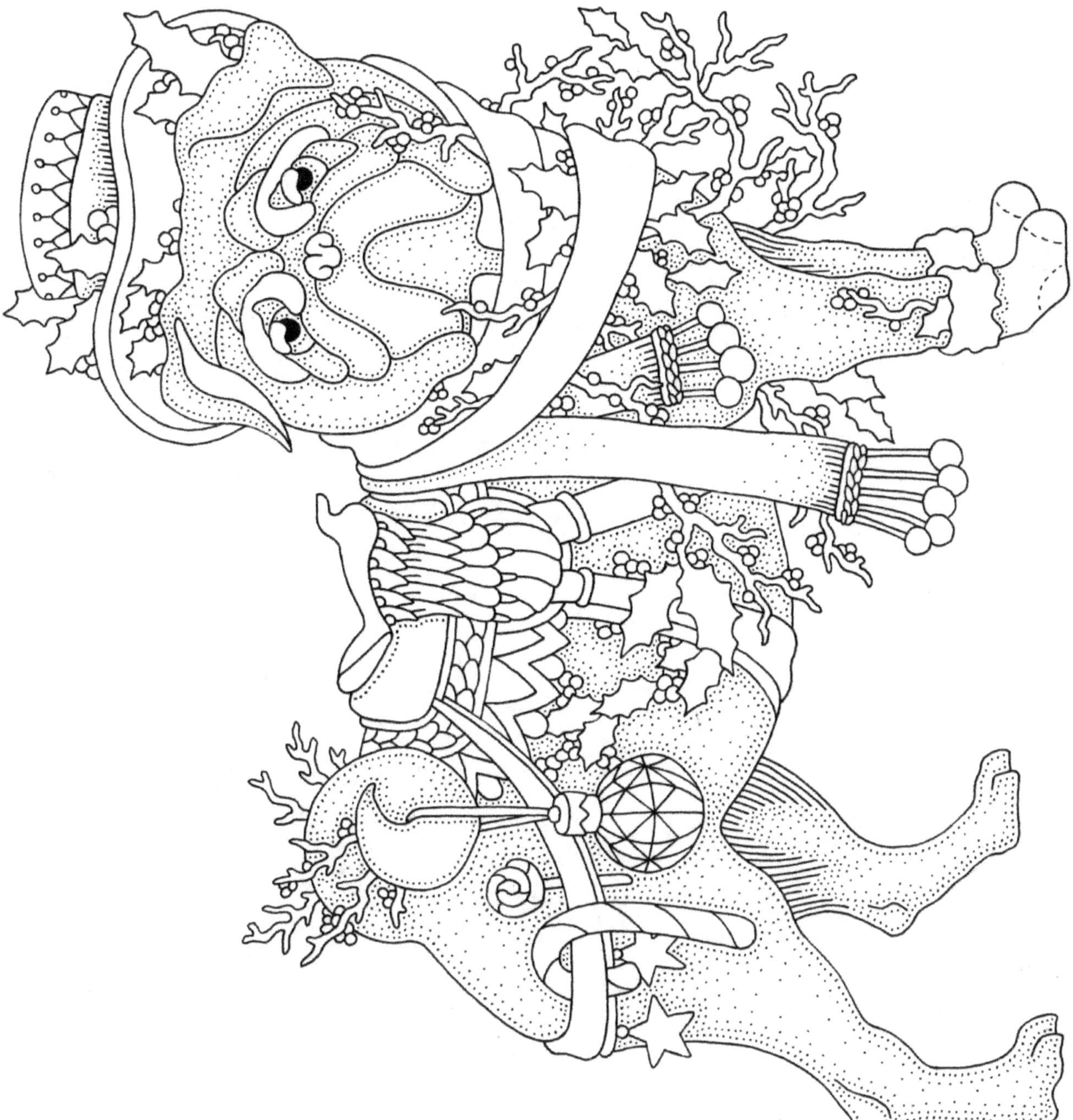

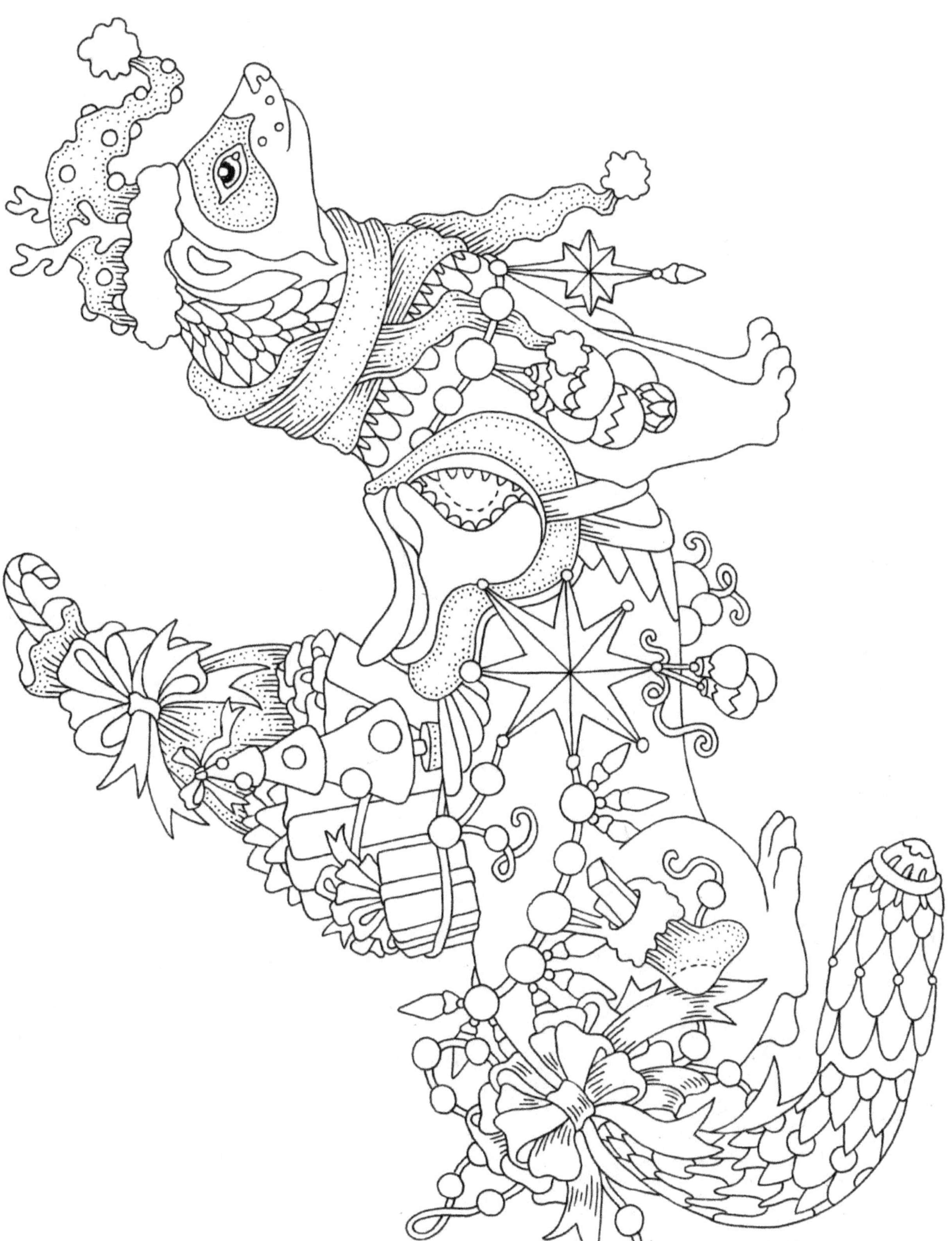

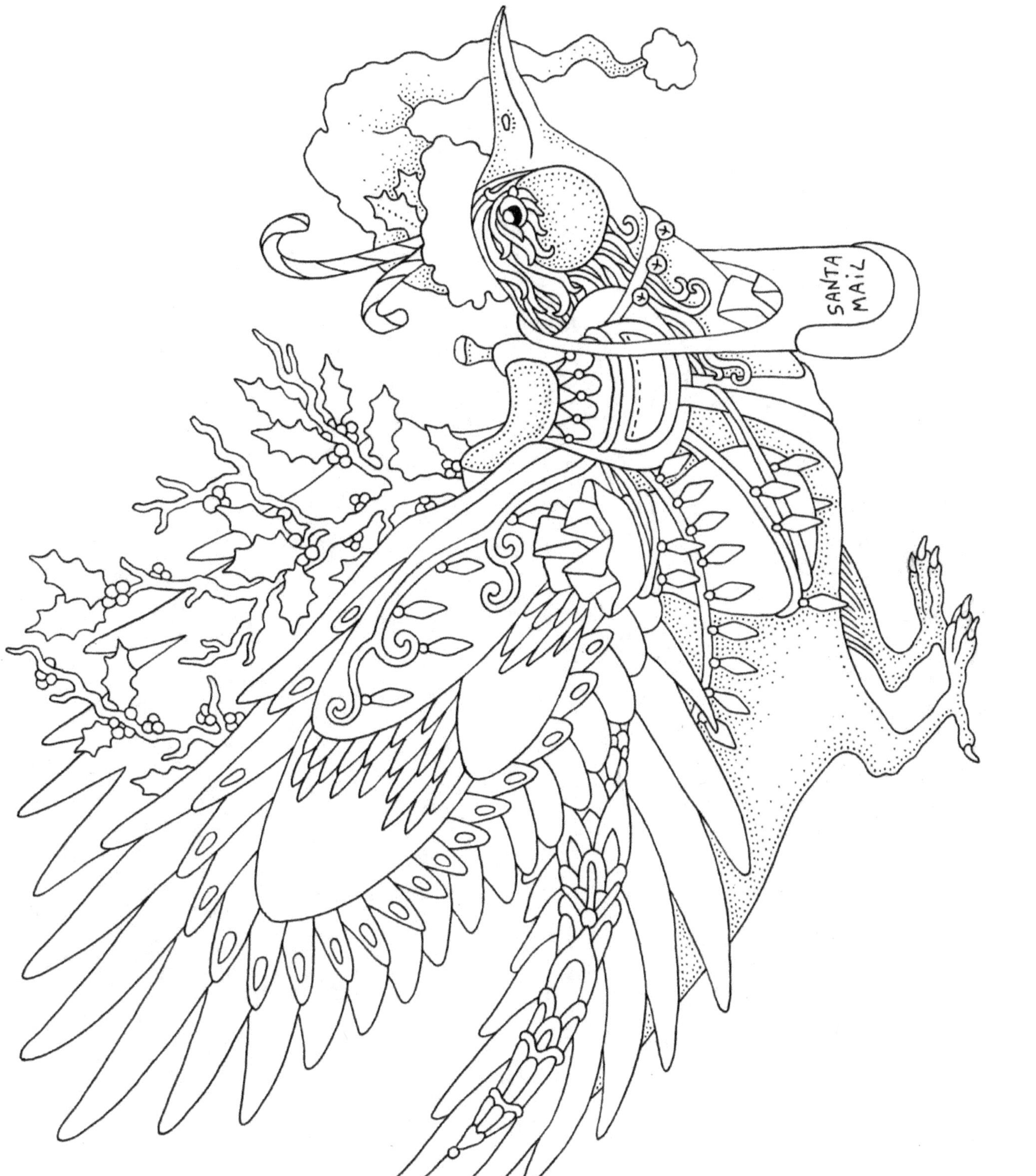
SANTA
MAIL

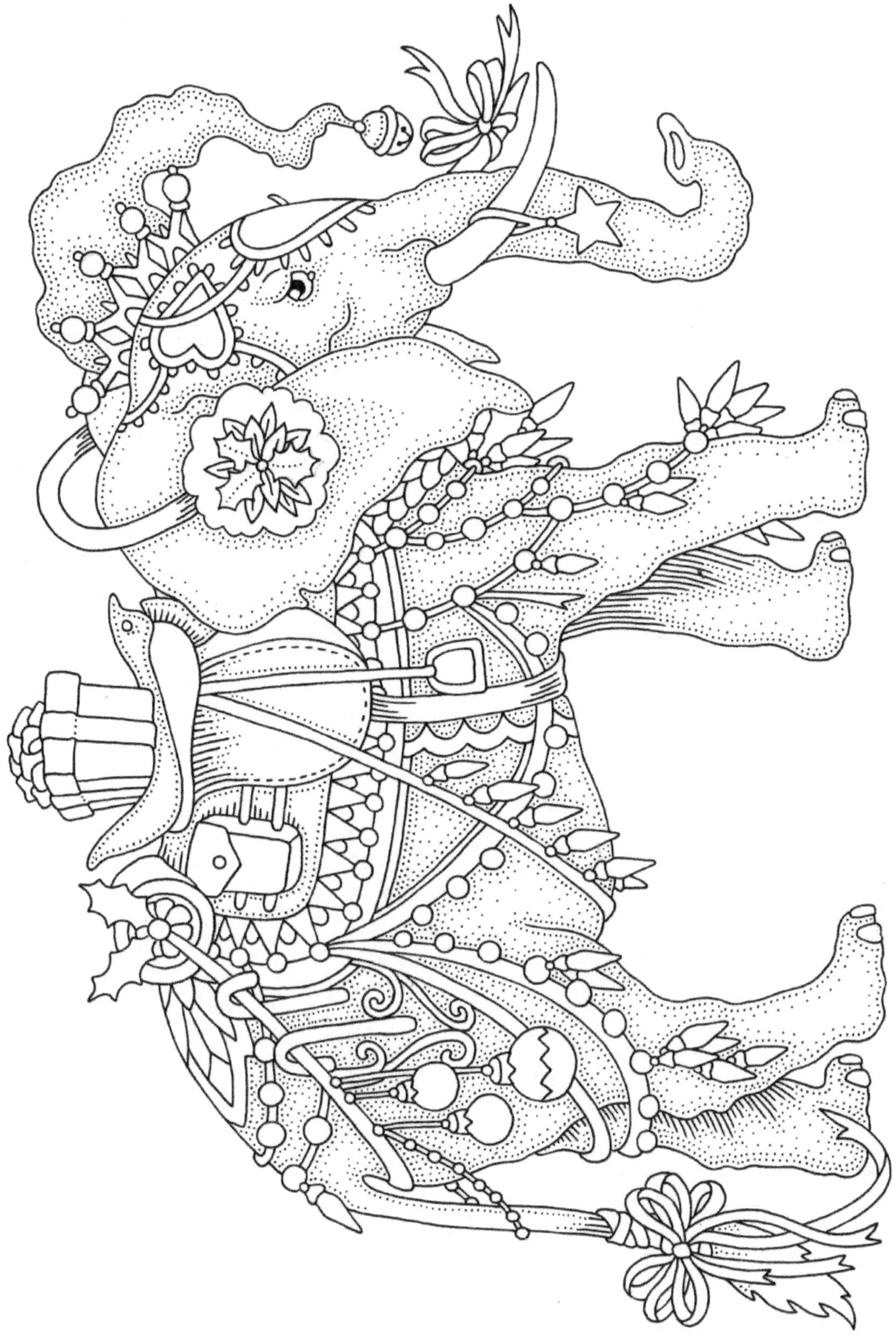

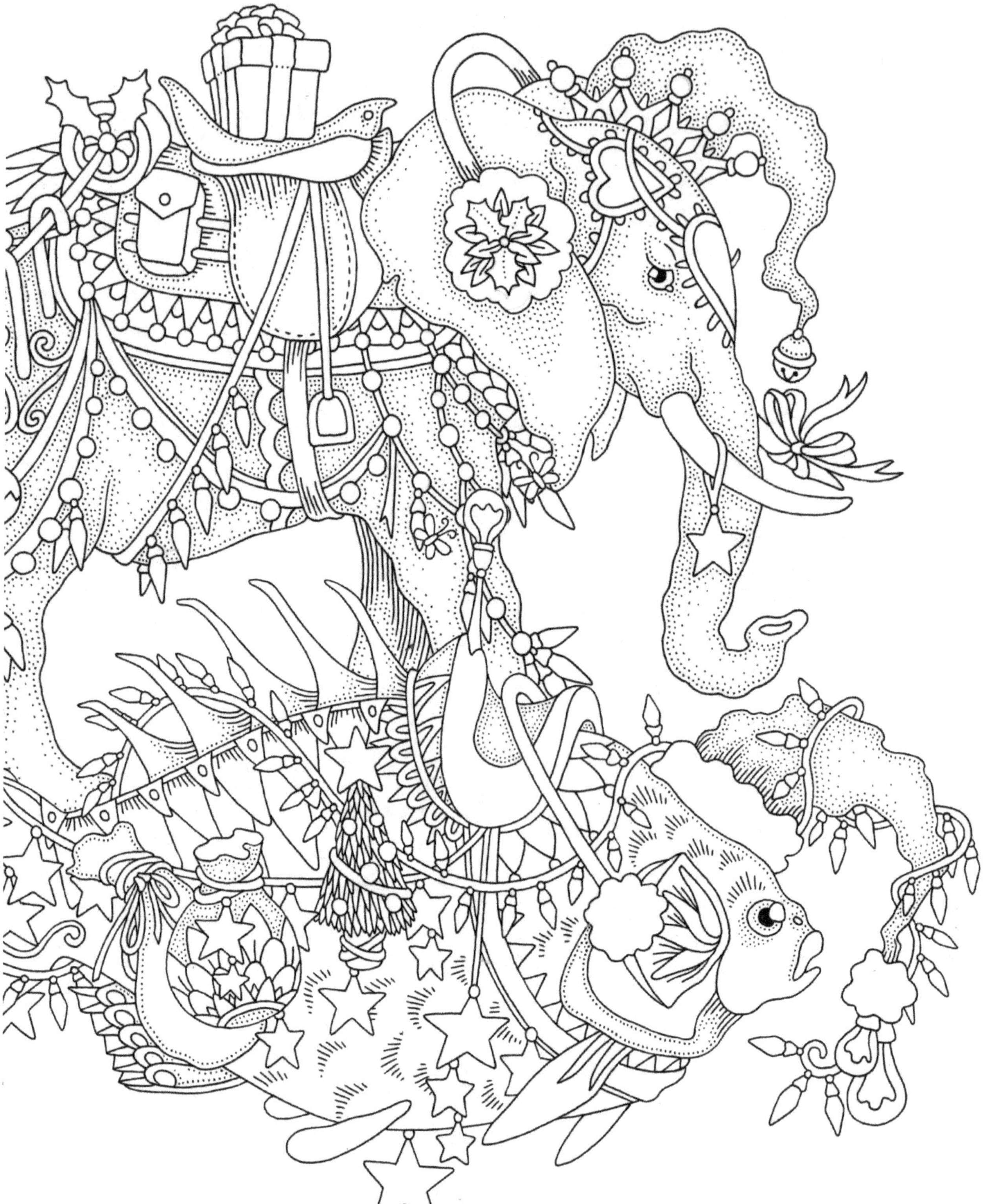

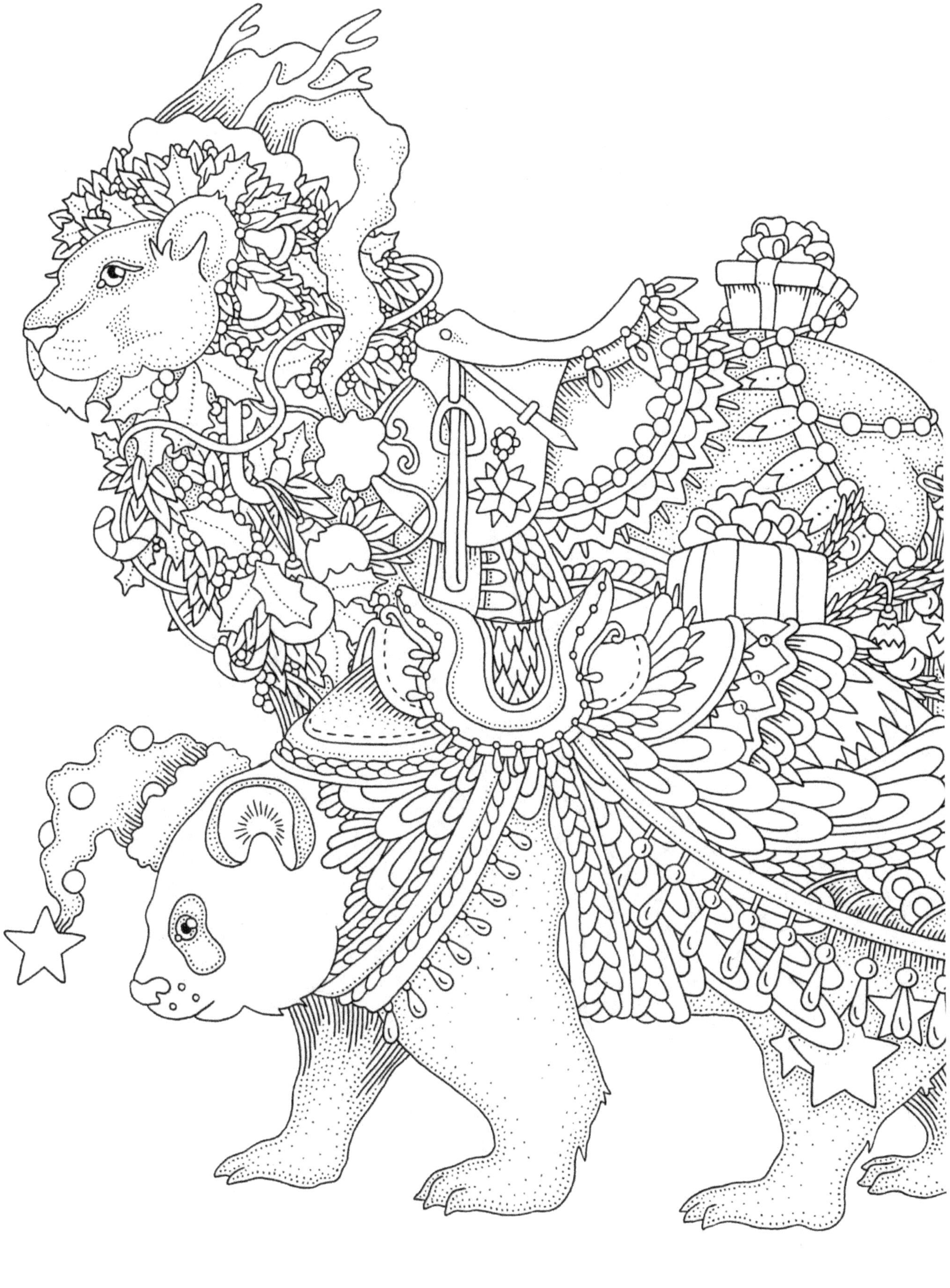

www.ingramcontent.com/pod-product-compliance
Lightning Source LLC
Chambersburg PA
CBHW060005230526
45472CB00008B/1949
* 9 7 8 1 9 7 9 9 2 0 2 0 9 *